1000
word puzzles

Philip Carter

T0150203

D&B PUBLISHING
www.dandbpublishing.com

First published in 2010 by D&B Publishing.

Some puzzles in this book have previously been published in *200 Word Puzzles* (D&B Publishing 2003), *How to Solve Word Puzzles* (D&B Publishing 2005) and *Boost Your Interview Test Performance* (D&B Publishing 2005).

British Library Cataloguing-in-Publication Data
A catalogue record for this book is available from the British Library.

ISBN: 978-1-904468-46-2

All sales enquiries should be directed to D&B Publishing:
Tel: 01273 711443, e-mail: info@dandbpublishing.com,
Website: www.dandbpublishing.com

Cover design by Horatio Monteverde.
Printed and bound in the US by Versa Press.

CONTENTS

INTRODUCTION

Good words cost nothing but are worth much.
Thomas Fuller

The English language has evolved from an awkward native dialect, the tongues of various invaders and the importation of other foreign words.

The result is a language consisting of some half a million words and spoken by an estimated 400 million people throughout the world. Because of the way it has evolved, the English language is rich in alternative words, such as work and labour, friendly and amicable, and is one of the most expressive of all tongues.

People delight in playing with words – pulling words apart, reconstructing them in different guises, arranging them in clever patterns and finding hidden meanings within them.

Verbal intelligence is a measurement of your capacity to use language in order to express yourself, comprehend written text and understand other people. It is said that to have mastery of language is to have the ability to produce order out of chaos and that command of vocabulary is a true measure of intelligence.

The English language is a bottomless treasure chest of delight and in this book I have set out to entertain you, and give your brain a thorough work-out, in a wide selection of different types of word puzzles of varying degrees of difficulty.

Philip Carter

Change one letter only in each word below to form a familiar phrase.

kelp it ban

Complete the words below so that the same two letters that end the first word start the second word and the same two letters that end the second word start the third word etc. The same two letters that end the ninth word are also the first two letters of the first word, to complete the circle.

```
**LL**
**CA**
**PO**
**DA**
**AS**
**MI**
**BU**
**TE**
**AN**
```

PEERS MEET SECT is an anagram of which two words that are similar in meaning?

If H T G T represents the phrase *here today gone tomorrow*, what phrase is represented by the letters: I N R B I P ?

Work from letter to adjacent letter horizontally and vertically, but not diagonally, to spell out a 12-letter word. You must find the starting point and provide the missing letter.

```
A   N   U   *
M   O   E   R
E   L   B   A
```

Change one letter only in each word below to form a familiar phrase.

FROG HERD SO TOP

Which two words are closest in meaning?

upstart, placard, posterior, parvenu, janitor, echo

The clue *disposed of precious metal to purchaser* leads to which pair of rhyming words?

Of the following five words, four have a common theme. Which is the odd one out?

taffeta, garotte, hessian, nankeen, gingham

Of the following five words, four have a common theme. Which is the odd one out?

shilling, guinea, bezant, dime, cachelot

From the following six words select the two which are opposite in meaning.

dank, original, adjust, diffidence, dry, humility

The clue *tiny storm* leads to which pair of rhyming words?

The clue *disagree with direction* leads to which pair of rhyming words?

The clue *traveller slightly under the influence of alcohol* leads to which pair of rhyming words?

VERGER   is to   church as a
TYCOON   is to   (bursar, jobber, gaffer, businessman, teller)

Take two of the three-letter elements and combine them to make a six-letter word which fits the keyword definition.

FISH   (MUL, CUT, TUR, LER, TAL, BOT)

Use each letter of the phrase PERCEIVE HOLY ARCH once each only to spell out three types of fruit.

From the following six words select the two which are closest in meaning.

inexact, heedless, indolent, imprudent, immodest, reproachful

In the phrase below the first letter of each word has been removed as well as spacing. What is the phrase?

HEWHEUD

GORY CERAMICS is an anagram of which two words that are similar in meaning?

WARDER   is to   prison as a
AUGUSTE   is to   (theatre, circus, pantomime, busker, ministral)

What is the longest word in the English language that can be produced from the ten letters below? No letter may be used more than once.

METWLACYIF

Place the same word in front of each of these words to make five new words.

```
(- - - -)        CARD
                 AGE
                 MAN
                 HASTE
                 BOX
```

Insert two letters in each set of brackets so that they complete a word when tacked onto the letters on the left and start another word when placed in front of the letters on the right. The correct letters in the brackets must spell out an eight-letter word when read downwards in pairs.

```
CO (**) SO
GRA (**) ASE
GR (**) LE
PO (**) CH
```

Use every letter of the phrase below once each only to spell out two types of dog.

BLEAK AGED PRISONER

Which bracketed word is most similar in meaning to the key word?

INDEMNIFY   (accuse, besot, compensate, confused, injure)

A familiar phrase has been split into three letter groups which have been arranged in alphabetical order. What is the phrase?

est   lou   lth   ops   pul   tal

HER NINTH AGE is an anagram of which phrase (4, 2, 5)   Clue persevere

Which bracketed word is most opposite in meaning to the key word?

HUMANE   (tedious, cruel, depressing, passion, uncouth)

What is a QUOIN?

(a)   Ancient drink
(b)   Coin
(c)   External angle of a building
(d)   Joint of meat

SCULPTER   is to   figures as
TAILOR   is to   (suits, dresses, hats, fashion, clothes)

CAR, MAD, BIT, TON, DEN, ?

What word comes next?

Apart from each having six letters, what do the following words have in common?

repair, stroke, sacrum, retype

Think of an entertainment legend from days of long ago, who was a star of stage and movies. The legend's surname is 8-letters long. Transfer the first four letters of this legend's name from beginning to end to produce something which might inflame my gout. Who is the entertainment legend I am thinking of?

Which bracketed word is most similar in meaning to the key word?

PATRON   (advocate, enemy, ancestry, fussy, indigence)

DID TRUCE is an anagram of two 'this and that' words CUT, DRIED (cut and dried). THREE SWOTS is an anagram of which two other this and that words?

Only one group of five letters below can be arranged to spell out a five-letter word in the English language. Find the word.

DICON
NERHO
AOPKT
CUPGA
UFALE
AGCIT

Insert a word in the brackets so that it completes a word or phrase when tacked onto the word on the left and completes another word or phrase when placed in front of the word on the right.

lucky ( ) offensive

Remove a letter from a tactician to leave a power tool for smoothing wood.

Change one letter only in each word below to form a familiar phrase.

LACE NO FAME

Insert a mythical Greek character onto the bottom line to complete eight 3-letter words reading downwards.

A	T	F	A	Y	P	H	W
S	O	A	R	O	A	O	A
*	*	*	*	*	*	*	*

Insert two letters in each set of brackets so that they complete a word when tacked onto the letters on the left and start another word when placed in front of the letters on the right. The correct letters in the brackets must spell out an eight-letter word when read downwards in pairs.

WA (**) CK
PO (**) GE
ALL (**) HER
EP (**) ON

Complete the four words with the aid of the clues. The letters *xyz* in each word are the same three letters which spell out a three-letter word.

xyz***	bovine
*xyz**	damage or destroy
**xyz*	find
***xyz	type of grape

What is the meaning of THRENODY?

a. the sill of a window
b. thin in diameter

c. a song of lamentation
d. not prudent

The object outside the brackets always has two of the features inside the brackets. Identify which two

Oil painting (hook, frame, colour, signature, landscape)

GEN   REAL

Insert two three-letter words that are opposite in meaning into the groups of letters above (one each) to produce two new words.

In the phrase below the first letter of each word has been removed as well as spacing. What is the phrase?

CTOURGE

Use each letter of the phrase KAKAPO OR ALKALOID once each only to spell out three types of bear.

up, out, copy

Which word below has something in common with the words above?

part   east   remit   down   cage

A familiar phrase has been split into three letter groups which have been arranged in alphabetical order. What is the phrase?

act   der   eak   ion   lou   nwo   rds   ssp   tha

Find one word in this paragraph. It appears only once, its first letter being the eighth letter after a certain vowel. This same vowel is the tenth letter to appear after its last letter.

O   *OM*   *AT*   *I*

Complete the above words by adding a familiar sequence of letters to the beginning of the words, and the same sequence, but in reverse to the end of the words.

What is the hidden message concealed in the following words:

aniseed, joyously, bath, antenna, chipmunk

Which one of the following is an anagram of CHITTY CHITTY BANG BANG?

CHANCY BATTING BY NIGHT   CATCH BITCHY GNAT BY GIN
ANY TIGHT ITCHING CABBY   ITCHY BITCH 'N' BATTY GNAT
ANY ITCHY TIGHT BBC GNAT   NINTH CATCH BY BATTY GIT

Find two of the three words: that can be paired to form an anagram that is a synonym of the remaining word. For example, with LEG - MEEK - NET, the words LEG and NET form an anagram of GENTLE, which is a synonym of the remaining word, MEEK.

        early – purer – tamely

Below are the names of eight ancient Greeks. Take one letter from each in turn to spell out the name of another ancient Greek.

Aesop, Zeno, Euclid, Homer, Thales, Antiphon, Aristotle, Diodorus

Find a common theme to the words below.

nail, green, band, work, way, bite

Pair the ten words below to produce five phrases which are all oxymorons.

inside, fortune, student, heavyweight, difference, small, teacher, light, out, same

From the following six words select the two which are opposite in meaning.

modest, penury, revenge, acute, limpid, plenty

DENTIST   is to   teeth as
APIARIST   is to   (insects, monkeys, bees, kittens, lions)

Which two words that sound alike but are spelled differently mean invoiced and construct?

Complete the four words with the aid of the clues. The letters *xyz* in each word are the same three letters which spell out a three-letter word.

xyz***   puncture
*xyz**   each
**xyz*   sword
***xyz   bird

PATRONAGE is to ORANGE as CAPACITOR is to?

Add a letter to a chessman to produce a crustacean.

Take two of the three-letter elements and combine them to make a six-letter word which fits the keyword definition.

BIRD   (PUF, CAN, FIM, PIG, ARY, OIN)

land, line, mast, sail

Which word below has something in common with the words above?

park, trap, calm, draw, stay

Which film star arranged comedial laughs?

GAY AND SULLEN is an anagram of which familiar phrase (4,4,4)

Clue: the good old days

If H T G T = here today gone tomorrow, what phrase is represented by the initials: M H M L W

Use each letter of the phrase FIERCELY SPOOK ANT once each only to spell out three types of hawk.

Remove a letter from a form of address to leave a cheapskate.

NAKED EDEN is an anagram of which two words that sound alike but are spelled differently and have different meanings?

Complete the hyphenated word below.

* * * F F – F * * *

If 9L of a C is nine lives of a cat, can you decode the following?

13 S on the A F

Place the same word in front of each of these words to make five new words.

(- - - - -) HAUL
HAND
FALL
SIGHTED
NESS

Select two words that are synonyms, plus an antonym of these two synonyms, from the list of words below.

molecular, toxic, septic, calm, cohesive, durable, safe

LESSER AVALANCHE is an anagram of which London sporting event (7, 1, 7)

If meat in a river (3 in 6) is T(HAM)ES can you find a rodent in a packing case (3 in 5)?

Which two words meaning a pier and glide on runners rhyme with each other but have no letters in common?

The answer you are looking for to solve the charade below is a nine-letter word.

A position to be with a portable shelter which is electrically charged.

mute, para, mala, eral, wolf, jack, ural, tune, tain.

Pair up two of the bits above to produce a breed of sled dog.

From the following six words select the two which are closest in meaning.

hinder, obvious, anticipate, casual, manifest, obduracy

Use every letter of the phrase TRUNCATED AS A BRAN TUB once each only to produce three foodstuffs which are usually the same colour.

What is PROGENY?

(a)	Malted hops	(c)	Offspring
(b)	Group of snails	(d)	Ruling by Parliament

Which letter does not belong in the list?

B R C A O T

Insert two letters in each set of brackets so that they complete a word when tacked onto the letters on the left and start another word when placed in front of the letters on the right. The correct letters in the brackets must spell out a six-letter word when read downwards in pairs.

        TI (**) SK
        LA (**) AM
        DU (**) OP

Which two words are the odd ones out?

nil, scruple, hardtop, trouper, due, mop, scrappy, rue, ado, adjured, entitle, cap

Which three-letter word in the English language forms two other words, unrelated in meaning, when less and ness are added to the end of it?

Clue: bon mot

What short phrase is suggested by the arrangement of letters below?

    RE – NDEER

Complete the hyphenated word below

* * * * * R – S T * * *

RI *LO* *HI* *EE* *AS* *IE* *ON* *IG*

Add a familiar sequence to complete the eight words above.

krl, hoy, aent, cule, bch, aord, foy

Insert a familiar sequence into the letter arrangements above to produce seven words.

M
I
D
D
L
E

Add the following words to the list above to produce six new words.

arch   over   edge   spat   rift   raft
know   less   frog   snow   ally   spin

Use each letter of the phrase DARK FOX DROOLS MOON once each only to spell out three cities worldwide beginning with the letter O.

The object outside the brackets always has two of the features inside the brackets. Identify which two

Church (clock, path, font, gate, sexton)

What letter follows:

T N O R F O T K C A ?

Use the letters of the phrase NOTICEABLY CHIC CAR once each only to spell out three types of transport.

Insert a word in the brackets so that it completes a word or phrase when tacked onto the word on the left and completes another word or phrase when placed in front of the word on the right.

Head   (   )   pipe

artistic, ? , startled, repartee, ramparts, stalwart

What word is missing?

compartment, partaken , quarters, licences, mistaken

Place two letters in each set of brackets so that they finish the word on the left and start the word on the right. The letters inserted when read downwards in pairs must spell out an eight-letter word.

BA (**) NT
DU (**) AS
RI (**) IP
RE (**) CH

BLUE	is to	navy as
RED	is to	(scarlet, indigo, sienna, olive, saffron)

Place two letters in each set of brackets so that they finish the word on the left and start the word on the right. The letters inserted when read downwards in pairs must spell out an eight-letter word.

WE (**) IC
AC (**) LP
TA (**) SS
LI (**) FT

Which bracketed word is most similar in meaning to the key word?

BURNISHED   (elegant, refined, approached, shrewd, brightened)

Which of the following is not an anagram of a type of vegetable?

cash pin   drain man
take choir   cult tee
spin rap   war secrets

CRON   FE   BUSS

Insert three 4-letter words into the middle of the letter arrangements to produce three words. The three 4-letter words inserted must form a familiar phrase.

Arrange the letters of each word below to find three words which all begin with the letters CU, for example CU + BLEAR = CURABLE

TRIAL
TYRES
DARTS

T A N M O

Add a vowel to the five letters above, and then rearrange the six letters to produce a word in the English language.

In an endeavour to occasion an impediment that may lead to difficulty I am tossing an instrument used for securing small metal blocks, causing it to alight within the confines of mechanism in progress.

What am I doing?

Of the following five words, four have a common theme. Which is the odd one out?

saltpetre, polythene, sulphur, acetate, lumbago

Of the following five words, four have a common theme. Which is the odd one out?

shallot, wimbrel, spinach, marrow, cherry

Complete the seven sins below with the aid of the clues provided:

SIN******	honesty of mind
*SIN*****	another name for mica
SIN**	intimate
SIN	with humour
****SIN**	former name for Ethiopia
*****SIN*	disconcerting
******SIN	US state, known as the Badger State

From the following six words select the two which are opposite in meaning.

boorish, derange, itinerary, quarrel, imperial, civilised

Below are five words related to the game of cards. Take one letter from each in turn to spell out another word associated with the game of cards.

shuffle, deal, deuce, solitaire, hand

try, ache, cake

Which word below has something in common with the words above?

camp, handle, winter, autumn, finish

Place two letters in each set of brackets so that they finish the word on the left and start the word on the right. The letters inserted when read downwards in pairs must spell out a ten-letter word.

SA (**) SH
AR (**) UG
LE (**) ON
CH (**) ED
FO (**) LY

Take two of the three-letter elements and combine them to make a six-letter word which fits the keyword definition.

DOGS   (BAS, POO, SER, DLE, COL, LIA)

HOT TOUCHES is an anagram of which two words that sound alike but are spelled differently and have different meanings?

Place a word in the brackets that means the same as the definitions outside the brackets.

Circlet   (   )   peal

Which bracketed word is most opposite in meaning to the key word?

NIGGARD   (spendthrift, churl, skinflint, delicate, common)

What word is indicated below?

 ⊤ M

The answer to each clue is a rhyming pair of words, for example, unhappy young man = sad lad

an extended step
frighten a Prime minister
without support
grey matter depletion
South African mammal's histrionics

more crafty member of a religious order
elite squad
flip quickly through scheme
grasp lash
restrict lovemaking

Remove a letter from a harsh noise to leave an erect leafless flower stalk.

Place the same word in front of each of these words to make five new words.

(- - - -)   SOME
              BALL
              GUN
              HELD
              BAG

DID TRUCE is an anagram of two 'this and that' words CUT, DRIED (cut and dried). CHICO SPOKE is an anagram of which two other this and that words?

ALE   RIE   IMOR

What four-letter word can be inserted into the letter arrangements above to form three words?

Use every letter of the phrase FINISHED CRUMBLIER MEAT to produce three jobs or professions.

Complete the four words with the aid of the clues. The letters *xyz* in each word are the same three letters which spell out a three-letter word.

xyz***	haphazard
*xyz**	colour
**xyz*	fallible
***xyz	exceeded in pace

Select two words that are synonyms, plus an antonym of these two synonyms, from the list of words below.

disconcerted, candid, observant, apathetic, agog, afflicted, enthralled

What connects the words marzipan, dahlia, oxide, error, sermon, keynote, bronze, brazen, alkali, onion, sell, amalgam

If meat in a river (3 in 6) is T(HAM)ES can you find the pitch in a type of salmon (3 in 7)?

Complete the following palindrome by inserting the missing word/s:

Niagara, O **** again

What is PODAGRA?

(a)	Gout	(c)	Weapon
(b)	Summer house	(d)	Sweet wine

Only one of the groups of six letters below can be arranged into a 6 - letter word in the English language. Find the word.

MUTEBO   HENILT   RILBAC
LORCIN   LORMTA
TABONE   OFNIWE

A phrase, which it is advised you should never do, has been sliced up into 3-letter bits and the bits then rearranged in alphabetical order. Can you reconstruct the saying?

For example: find the quote would be split into fin/d th/e qu/ote and the bits rearranged into alphabetical order thus: dth, equ, fin, ote

emo, hor, ift, kag, loo, nth, sei, uth

Arrange the sixteen words in pairs to produce eight hyphenated words:

BOARD	CANDLE	CORNER	CHILD
DRIVER	FIRST	GHOST	MORTAR
PRIZE	SCHOOL	SCREW	STICK
STONE	STRING	WINNER	WRITER

Test Three: Question 36

Each number represents the same letter in each set. Find the six words that are all anagrams of each other.

1234	3124	1243
3421	4213	2143

Test Three: Question 37

From the following six words select the two which are closest in meaning.

persevere, enduring, clever, maternal, maintain, pertinent

Test Three: Question 38

Which two words that are pronounced the same but spelled differently mean: attendance and donations?

Test Three: Question 39

Find the answer to the cryptic clue below which is an anagram contained within the clue.

Disguised mutable moans during a night walk.

Test Three: Question 40

Select two words that are synonyms, plus an antonym of these two synonyms, from the following list.

impassable, evasive, orbicular, dangerous, circuitous, easy, direct

In each of the following change one letter only from each word to produce a well-known phrase, for example chose ball = c**l**ose **c**all

add ode cut

of tie toil

Carl tie tone

put any cried

on deer later

keen in ewe put

otter dish so cry

lad town tie lad

I kiss in US food am I milk

mass she back

Which bracketed word is most similar in meaning to the key word?

PENURY   (astute, discreet, poverty, descent, charming)

The object outside the brackets always has two of the features inside the brackets. Identify which two

Sea (boats, tide, estuary, waves, pier)

Which politician disturbs crazed leghorn gnawers?

Remove a letter from a witty humorist to leave a gambler.

Which two seven-letter words meaning abounding in words and take notice are anagrams of each other?

Insert a word in the brackets so that it completes a word or phrase when tacked onto the word on the left and completes another word or phrase when placed in front of the word on the right.

Pin   (   )   out

Insert a girl's name into the bottom line to complete nine 3 - letter words reading downwards.

H	S	N	F	O	T	S	R	C
U	E	O	O	W	O	K	A	U
*	*	*	*	*	*	*	*	*

If meat in a river (3 in 6) is T(HAM)ES can you find a weapon in someone who does not behave seriously (5 in 7)?

Which bracketed word is most similar in meaning to the key word?

DAUNT   (barren, dismay, bewilder, gloom, bold)

The answer you are looking for to solve the charade below is an eleven-letter word.

This kitty with a human blood type was declared deranged.

Complete the paragraph with the six missing words. The first word you are looking for is a four-letter word and every other word you are looking for commences with this same four-letter word.

Now that I'm a ****, people tend to *****. I often ******** to escape to another world. When I was a ******* and all ******-****, I would dream of *******.

Which two words are closest in meaning?

sated, oceanic, saturated, pelagic, expansive, expendable

IBEX is to PILE as CHEER is to ?????

Place two letters in each set of brackets so that they finish the word on the left and start the word on the right. The letters inserted when read downwards in pairs must spell out an eight-letter word.

JA (**) NY
HO (**) AT
TU (**) ME
LA (**) ON

Insert a word in the brackets so that it completes a word or phrase when tacked onto the word on the left and completes another word or phrase when placed in front of the word on the right.

Coal   (   )   bowl

O   A**   *E*E*   **O   *L*   *O   *E*R*

Complete the well-known saying above.

Solve the anagram below which is of three connected words. For example hop, skip, jump.

CALL STOCKBROKER

bantam, paper, over

Which word below has something in common with all the words above?

Spider, fly, cockroach, ant, beetle

Complete the following palindrome by inserting the missing word/s:

Dennis and **** sinned

Which bracketed word is most opposite in meaning to the key word?

OBSTINATE   (mystic, docile, encroaching, noisy, hindrance)

Find two of the three words: that can be paired to form an anagram that is a synonym of the remaining word. For example, with LEG - MEEK - NET, the words LEG and NET form an anagram of GENTLE, which is a synonym of the remaining word, MEEK.

rue – get – crop

From the following six words select the two which are opposite in meaning.

larceny, sensual, vigour, parody, shortage, honesty

Take two of the three-letter elements and combine them to make a six-letter word which fits the keyword definition.

REPTILES   (LIS, IGU, ARD, PYT, HOD, ANA)

In the phrase below the first letter of each word has been removed as well as spacing. What is the phrase?

IENAIT

star   care   late   brat   meal   chop

Add a familiar series of letters to the above words to produce six new words.

Find two of the three words: that can be paired to form an anagram that is a synonym of the remaining word. For example, with LEG - MEEK - NET, the words LEG and NET form an anagram of GENTLE, which is a synonym of the remaining word, MEEK.

Frenetic – bogus – out

Start at one of the stars and finish at the other and work from letter to adjacent letter horizontally and vertically, but not diagonally, to spell out a well-known proverb. Every letter is used, once each only.

```
                *
A     M    T    R    O
N     O    O    B    T
Y     S    S    E    H *
C     K    P    H    T
O     O    O    I    L
```

When you have solved the above puzzle try to find another proverb (4, 5, 4, 5, 4) which means exactly the opposite of the one above, by solving the anagram:

      mark my shaking hand-towel

ERA, CAN, CAM, - - -

Place the above in the correct order and insert the correct word missing from the list.

From the following six words select the two which are closest in meaning.

succour, constant, remedy, agitate, pause, faithful

What are CONGERIES?

a. a linked series
b. a random collection or heap of things

c. late evening prayers
d. baptismal robes

SMELL   is to   nose as
BALANCE   is to   (ankles, feet, hands, fingers, hair)

Which bracketed word is most similar in meaning to the key word?

EGRESS   (exit, dirge, effusion, simple, vain)

Using the letters of WORDPLAY no more than twice each, what 9-letter word in the English language can be produced?

What is the proverb below?

one S D M a S

Which word is in the wrong column?

Bell	Hot
Chip	Moon
Print	Wood
	Carpet

What four-letter word goes behind test, inner and torpedo?

Select two words that are synonyms, plus an antonym of these two synonyms, from the following list.

accede, destroy, refuse, protect, moderate, assuage, conserve

Place the same word in front of each of these words to make five new words.

(- - -)   BOY
                CASE
                ROT
                TED
                PET

What is a PISCINE?

(a)	Drink	(c)	Relating to a fish
(b)	Fever	(d)	Flower

Fill in the missing consonants to find four words similar in meaning.

```
* * A I *
E * U * A * E
I * * * * U * *
* O A * *
```

Which bracketed word is most similar in meaning to the key word?

MARROW   (boundary, marine, brand, morass, substance)

Change the first word into the second word by finding a link at each stage, for example, the word HAND can be changed to GLOVE by proceeding: HAND – OUT – FOX – GLOVE.
Go from SIDE to SIDE

```
S I D E
* I * E
* *
* A * E
* * L *
T * * *
* * P
S I D E
```

U	Z	C	W
H	K	Q	J
P	X	T	V
Y	M	G	R

Only ten letters of the alphabet do not appear in the array above. What 10 - letter phrase (3, 2, 5) can they be arranged to spell out?
Clue: Does the fakir derive any comfort from this?

Add one letter, not necessarily the same letter, to each word, at the beginning, middle or end, to find seven words that all have something in common.

how, rat, loop, big, put, bare, cane

In each of the following groups of three words your task is to find two of the three that can be paired to form an anagram of one word, which is a synonym of the word remaining. For example, LEG - MEEK - NET. The words LEG and NET are an anagram of GENTLE, which is a synonym of the remaining word - MEEK.

sorry - net - inept   sail - alike - rim
hasten - fan - suit   edit - exact - lead
able - finite - crop   lithe - sew - late

If meat in a river (3 in 6) is T(HAM)ES can you find a legume in a hat (3 in 7)?

MINERAL   (ENIGMA)   KINGDOM

Using the same rules as in the example above, what word should appear in the brackets below?

ASTAIRE   (* * * * * *)   TINWARE

Below are five synonyms of the word FRAGMENT. Take one letter from each in turn to spell out another synonym of fragment.

morsel, chip, scrap, particle, shred

Insert two letters in each set of brackets so that they complete the word on the left and start the word on the right. The letters inserted, when read downwards in pairs, should spell out an 8 - letter word.

```
TA ( * * ) RT
SI ( * * ) SK
MO ( * * ) AR
ME ( * * ) LY
```

What word is indicated by the clues below?

> second ballet
> centre of Chicago
> sixth former
> first offender
> non-starter
> satisfactory conclusion
> bottom end

What do the words; late, lease, added, raise and utter all have in common?

Solve the anagrams in brackets (all one word) to complete the quotations by Albert Einstein.

i. (aiming at ion) is more important than knowledge.
ii. The eternal mystery of the world is its (embryonic Philistine)
iii. (tango trivia) can not be held responsible for people falling in love.
iv) Reality is merely an illusion, albeit a very (prettiness) one.
v) The most beautiful thing we can experience is the (yum stories).

The object outside the brackets always has two of the features inside the brackets. Identify which two

Aeroplane (propeller, stewards, wheels, wings, pilot)

Insert a word in the brackets so that it completes a word or phrase when tacked onto the word on the left and completes another word or phrase when placed in front of the word on the right.

knee   (   )   sea

Use every letter of the phrase PURGE CAPITAL ROMP once each only to spell out three types of fruit.

Solve the following line by line to find a seven-letter word.

My first's in Uranus and also Saturn,
My second's in artist and also pattern,
My third is in wizard but not in toad,
My fourth is in sequence but not in code,

My fifth is in brightness but not in dark,
My sixth is in robin but not in lark,
My seventh's in watch but not in time,
You sometimes chase what's in this rhyme.

Insert a word in the brackets so that it completes a word or phrase when tacked onto the word on the left and completes another word or phrase when placed in front of the word on the right.

Lace   (   )   payer

cap, ace, pie, trot

Add a letter, not necessarily the same letter, to the beginning, middle or end of the words above to produce four new words on the same theme

Start with a tree (4 letters).
Change one letter to produce a liquid measure
Add a letter to produce a pigment
Change a letter to produce a holy man
Change a letter to produce an unbroken period of time when you can do something
Change a letter to produce a malodour
Remove a letter to produce a kitchen receptacle
Delete a letter to find a transgression
Change a letter to produce a fastener
Add a letter to obtain the same tree that you started out with

Solve the cryptic clue below. The answer is an anagram contained within the clue.

Confuse bold Alicia with devilish scheme.

Solve the anagram below which is of three connected words. For example hop, skip, jump.

HALT RANDOM DALEKS

Which bracketed word is most similar in meaning to the key word?

LANGUOR   (lassitude, wanton, sensual, vigour, energetic)

can, fan, old, rub, back, coal, sale

Add a letter, not necessarily the same letter, to the beginning, middle or end of the words above to produce seven new words on the same theme

Only one group below can be arranged to spell out a six-letter word in the English language. Find the word.

TRIALC	DULOVA	KEIPEM	ZROPEN
NETYPA	ADHICP	PECOLU	

Remove a letter from a proscenium to leave a wise man.

P	O	?	K	L	Y
M	U	N	?	E	E

What letters are missing?

Insert a word in the brackets so that it completes a word or phrase when tacked onto the word on the left and completes another word or phrase when placed in front of the word on the right.

Dumb (   )   owed

Solve the anagrams of familiar phrases, for example, atom slut (3, 5) clue: aggregate; answer: sum total.

i) damn genial (7, 3)   clue: top billing
ii) the piglets (5, 5)   clue: sweet dreams
iii) to undo ode (3, 3, 3)   clue: unconventional
iv) open oath (3, 1, 4)   clue: woebegone

From the following six words select the two which are opposite in meaning.

advocate, support, barter, entrest, hinder, tiresome

The answer to each clue is an anagram to be solved within the clue, for example, device destroys the cart (7) ; answer: ratchet (anagram of *the cart*; anagram indicator; destroys)

i. Charming transformation for turbulent Gulf race (8)
ii) Literary classifier rewrites glib hair probe mystery (13)
iii) Resting houses reconstructed with high morality (13)
iv) Spin trash crazily from one vessel to another (9)

Test Five: Question 12

Solve each anagram to find two phrases that are spelled differently but sound alike, as, for example, in the two phrases *a name, an aim*.

i. grape tea   Egypt era
ii. woken canon   not onion

Test Five: Question 13

Insert two words that are anagrams of each other to complete the sentence, as in the example: She removed the *stain* from her new *satin* blouse.

After a fiercely competitive bout the fencing master sent his ****** for ******.

Test Five: Question 14

Take two of the three-letter elements and combine them to make a six-letter word which fits the keyword definition.

FLOWER   (LUP, DAH, CRO, KUS, LIE, INE)

Test Five: Question 15

Solve the anagrams below. Every answer contains the letters S O L V E.
For example SOLVE + IT = VIOLETS

SOLVE + TIMES =
SOLVE + BLEAR =
SOLVE + NUDER =

Change the first word into the second word by finding a link at each stage, for example, the word HAND can be changed to GLOVE by proceeding: HAND – OUT – FOX – GLOVE.

Go from PAINT to COAT

```
P A I N T
* R * * H
* * *
* U * *
F * E *
* I L *
* O W * *
* O U * *
C O A T
```

Complete the following palindrome by inserting the missing word/s:

Now Ned I am a ****** nun, Ned I am a maiden won

Solve the anagrams below to, in each case, produce a short palindromic sentence, for example, opponents set = step on no pets.

sense lifeline (6/7)
mean neon moan (4, 2, 3, 3)
overdone Denver (5, 3, 2, 4)

Create two related 5 - letter words using each of the ten letters of the phrase   PORN HARLOT once each only.

Combine three of the 3-letter bits below to produce a word meaning POTHOLER.

mal, ail, ker, ban, spe, ere, lun, are, spe, syl

```
 *    *    *    *    *    *    *
 I    X    I    C    A    P    H
 N    A    P    E    T    A    U
 *    *    *    *    *    *    *
```

Insert two gemstones, to produce seven four-letter words reading downwards.

Combine *four* of the 3-letter bits below to produce a word meaning an AREA

tan, tip, ole, reh, oli, set, rop, ewe, met, all

Change one letter only in each word *and then change the order of the words* to form a familiar phrase.

FAT CAVE THEY WET

Place the same word in front of each of these words to make five new words.

(- - -) CERT
TEXT
CURRENT
SENT
TENT

51

Place a word in the brackets that means the same as the definitions outside the brackets.

Intend   (   )   penurious

What word is suggested by the US states below?

Arkansas, California, Nebraska

Of the following five words, four have a common theme. Which is the odd one out?

marquess, lord, baron, king, count

What is the longest English word that can be produced from the following ten letters?

MURDOPLENH

5   What is MESCAL?

     (a)   A dance
     (b)   Intoxicating drink
     (c)   Feverish state
     (d)   Gaudy dress

Each of the following is an anagram of a number. The numbers increase in value.

For example: evens = seven

fin feet (7)
the vitrify (6, 4)
set envy (7)

to hygiene (6, 3)
yet inherent (6, 5)
herded hunter (5, 7)

shouting death (5, 8)
fill tiny room (5, 7)

From the following six words select the two which are closest in meaning.

slack, inadequate, puny, slovenly, artful, trifling

Each book title is the clue to a word and the name of the book's author is an anagram of that work, for example, The Writer by A. Routh - answer: author

Confined to Bed by Sid P. Edison
My Daily Bread by Sean N. Scute
Turncoat by Pat Oates
Discriminating Palate by Meg Rout
Pigeonhole by Rosette Pye
Counter Intelligence by Angie Pose
Verbose by Ursula Gor

What is the meaning of GLACIS?

a. glazed or glossy
b. greyish or bluish green

c. a gentle slope
d. possessing knowledge

Only one group of five letters below can be arranged to spell out a five-letter word in the English language. Find the word.

MYEAK   BEOHP   LGCIA
ALGCI   TBOAL   JAPLO

Which bracketed word is most opposite in meaning to the key word?

GULLIBILITY   (blameless, innocence, sinful, astuteness, credulity)

Which inventor transposes lavish anode atoms?

What two word phrase meaning at this place is spelled exactly the same as a word meaning not in any place?

chin, bacon, based, cat, state

Insert a familiar sequence of letters into the above words to produce five new words

Of the following five words, four have a common theme. Which is the odd one out?

guitar, saxaphone, clarinet, trumpet, oboe

The object outside the brackets always has two of the features inside the brackets. Identify which two

Calendar (months, days, notes, picture, tide times)

Use each letter of the newspaper headline once each only to spell out in each case three of a kind.

Three gemstones:
Lazy Mob Departure

Three fruit:
Paper Pager Plea

Three animals:
No Lithosphere Lane

Which of the following is not an anagram of a country?

and ionise   big Laura   regain tan
lizard newts   saw nothing

Solve the anagram in brackets, each is a one-word answer, to complete the name of the breed of animal, for example, (need bare) Angus = Aberdeen Angus

(main Santa) possum   (pure aeon) bison
(cat brain) camel   (preen any) mountain dog
(sheer Soho) bat   (panto again) cavy
(lame ashy) terrier   (shirt scam) beetle

RICHTER   is to   earthquakes as
BEAUFORT   is to   (weather, wind, sunshine, storms, gales)

Solve the four anagrams, all are one-word answers, and then say what the four words have in common.

if yard   an slid   risk elk   or moan

Famous Name Anagrams – who are the following?

a) American singer born 1942 in Brooklyn, New York (6,9)
   DARN RABBI STARES

b) Portuguese navigator and explorer (9,8)
   DAMN FINE LARGE LAND

c) American tennis player born 1970 and winner of several major championships (5,6)
   DRAIN SEA GAS

d) Legendary female aviator born in Achison, Kansas in 1898 (6,7)
   MAIL EARTH AREA

The three clues refer to a synonym, an antonym and an anagram (*in no particular order*). Figure out the answer word in each case. For example: halt, post, start
Answer word: stop
Post (anagram), halt (synonym), start (antonym)

resumed, unnoticed, ended
fade, shimmer, singlet
thoughtful, desecration, negligent

Change one letter only in each word below *and then change the order of the words* to form a familiar phrase.

PUT TROTH WALL

Below are eight synonyms of the word NAIVE. Take one letter from each in turn to spell out another synonym of naive.

gullible, green, trusting, ingenuous, childlike, credulous, unworldly, simplistic

Complete the words below so that the same two letters that finish the first word start the second word and the same two letters that finish the second word start the third word etc. The same two letters that finish the fifth word also start the first word to complete the circle.

```
** IS **
** SS **
** NG **
** IR **
** OO **
```

Complete the following palindrome by inserting the missing word/s:

Snug & raw was I ere * *** war & guns

Which bracketed word is most similar in meaning to the key word?

CONTENTION   (hostility, restless, wakeful, vigilant, skittish)

HARD   is to   steel as
SOFT   is to   (glass, tiles, lead, cushions, diamonds)

What connects the second wife of Henry VIII, the Northern lights, a nuclear weapon, a character from the Arabian Nights and an instrument that measures pressure without using fluid?

Use each letter of the phrase CLOTH EARED CORPULENT APE-MEN once each only to find three things found in an office environment.

What does someone holding a degree with a tendency to hoodwink people and who is intellectually ahead, likely to have for a meal?

Change one letter only in each word below *and then change the order of the words* to form a familiar phrase.

HOLE SOME FROG

Which bracketed word is most similar in meaning to the key word?

YOKEL   (young lad, bumpkin, slave, childish, juvenile)

Find the answers to the clues below. All the answers are three-word phrases in which each of the three words in the phrase starts with the same letter.

Reprimand
Repeatedly
The entire planet
Read the clock

Which bracketed word is most opposite in meaning to the key word?

FEASIBLE   (timid, delightful, dread, impracticable, achievable)

Solve the anagram below which is of three connected words. For example hop, skip, jump.

GET FRENCH LITTER

From the following six words select the two which are opposite in meaning.

lessen, loth, shudder, bright, willing, variety

```
   *     *     *     *     *     *
   I     D     O     R     C     A
   S     E     O     I     H     I
   *     *     *     *     *     *
```

Insert two types of fish, one on the top line and one on the bottom line to produce six four-letter words reading downwards.

What is the longest word that can be produced from the ten letters below? No letter may be used more than once.

WYVPOAITLN

Take two of the three-letter elements and combine them to make a six-letter word which fits the keyword definition.

FRUIT   (DAM, SOM, BAN, ORA, NGI, ANA)

If meat in a river (3 in 6) is T(HAM)ES can you find a fruit in Mentha spicata (4 in 9)?

Select two words that are synonyms, plus an antonym of these two synonyms, from the following list.

flexible, dull, severe, protracted, empty, stringent, dazzling

SUGGESTED USE is an anagram of which two words that sound alike but are spelled differently and have different meanings?

Complete the four 6 - letter words so that the same two letters that finish the first word start the second word, the same two letters that finish the second start the third, the same two letters that finish the third start the fourth, and the same two letters that finish the fourth are the same two letters that start the first word, to complete the circle.

```
* * C U * *
* * B U * *
* * N N * *
* * A P * *
```

Which bracketed word is most opposite in meaning to the key word?

HARROWING   (revolting, repulsive, irascible, delightful, animated)

Change one letter only in each word below *and then change the order of the words* to form a familiar phrase.

BEAR SAY OAF

Which two words that are anagrams of each other mean cursed and urgent request?

BY   DED   SPED   MOE   DAGE

Insert the same four-letter word into the five groups of letters above to produce five words.

OUTLASTING ACORN is an anagram of which 15-letter word?

What is the longest word that can be produced from the letters below? No letter may be used more than once.

TYBNOLIARH

Place the same word in front of each of these words to make five new words.

(- - -)   GAIN
                    MAN
                    ON
                    ROW
                    BELL

KNIFE   is to   slash as
CUDGEL   is to   (beat, impale, sever, scratch, ram)

Solve the anagrams below. Every answer contains the letters S O L V E.

For example SOLVE + IT = VIOLETS

SOLVE + A =   SOLVE + C =
SOLVE + RAP =   SOLVE + N =

From the following six words select the two which are closest in meaning.

fortify, relinquish, hardihood, forebode, reinforce, favoured

Solve the following line by line to produce an eight-letter word:

My first is in probability but not in chance,
My second's in fortune but not enhance,
My third's in amusement but not in skill,
My fourth is in pleasure and also thrill,
My fifth is in careful but not in bold,
My sixth is in bought but not in sold,
My seventh is in steadfast and also strong,
My eighth's in enduring but not in wrong,
My all is for the plucky,
And you might just get lucky.

What is an ASKARI?

     (a)   A soldier   (c)   A dance
     (b)   A fruit   (d)   A fish

WE   BOR   SASED

Insert three 3-letter words into the middle of the letter arrangements to produce three words. The three 3-letter words inserted must form a familiar phrase.

Which Charles Dickens' novel creates the lousy chiropodist?

Insert a word in the brackets so that it completes a word or phrase when tacked onto the word on the left and completes another word or phrase when placed in front of the word on the right.

Hope   (   )   on

Change one letter only in each word below *and then change the order of the words* to form a familiar phrase.

TACK LOU PAN

Each of the following is an anagram of a number, for example evens = seven.

Each successive answer is a number which increases in value.

NO REFUTE
EVEN TENSE
TEENY TOWN

Which is the odd one out?

Postage stamp
Silent letter
Clerical error
Second chance
Liberty bell
Intelligence test

BISHOP   is to   chessboard as
PIRATE   is to   (island, high seas, peg leg, treasure chest, flag)

What two words are suggested by this doublet?

So very tender to the touch,
Turned round the god we love so much.

A
E
I
O
U

Add the following words to the list above to produce five new words.

lion, cell, deer, wish, lose, with, ball, ring, post, yell

Find two of the three words: that can be paired to form an anagram that is a synonym of the remaining word. For example, with LEG - MEEK - NET, the words LEG and NET form an anagram of GENTLE, which is a synonym of the remaining word, MEEK.

Sauce – endemic – up

Complete the palindromic phrase with the aid of the clue: students err

* * * * * S   S * * *   U *

Which two words meaning fashionably elegant and a short high-pitched noise rhyme with each other but have no letters in common?

Who are the gatecrashers at the girl's Christmas party below?

Sally, Andrea, Nathalie, Mitzi, Tanya, Anne, Christine, Kathleen, Lucy, Agatha, Ursula, Sonja

Solve the clue below to find a pair of words.

    W O * * * * R D

Labour diligently

DING ABAND

Insert two 4-letter words into the middle of the letter arrangements to produce two words. The two 4-letter words inserted must form a familiar phrase.

Which two words that are anagrams of each other mean consisting of two parts and intelligent?

The clue bald black bird leads to which pair of rhyming word?

What word is suggested by the group of elements below?

astatine, lanthanum, sulphur

Change the first word into the second word by finding a link at each stage, for example, the word HAND can be changed to GLOVE by proceeding: HAND – OUT – FOX – GLOVE.

Change FINGER to HAND

```
FINGER
* * I *
* O * I S *
* * *
HAND
```

Change one letter only in each word below *and then change the order of the words* to form a familiar phrase.

TIP TO TIE EVER

*	*	*	*	*	*
H	F	O	I	I	C
U	A	S	D	S	H
*	*	*	*	*	*

Insert two countries, one on the top line and one on the bottom line to produce six four-letter words reading downwards.

The three clues refer to a synonym, an antonym and an anagram (*in no particular order*). Figure out the answer word in each case. For example: halt, post, start
Answer word: stop
Post (anagram), halt (synonym), start (antonym)

singer, quit, enlist
base, drain, top
restful, placate, agitate

Solve the anagram in brackets to find the famous subject of this Clerihew.

Said (smudged in fur),
I'm full of chagrin,
There was no theme,
To last night's dream

Solve the anagram in brackets to find the famous subject of this Clerihew.

(mushy hardy viper),   Discovered Sodium,
Loved meat with gravy,   But hated the odium.

term, list, wave

Which word below has something in common with all the words above?

cheek, eye, hand, toe, finger

Find two of the three words: that can be paired to form an anagram that is a synonym of the remaining word. For example, with LEG - MEEK - NET, the words LEG and NET form an anagram of GENTLE, which is a synonym of the remaining word, MEEK.

       invite – probe – stage

Solve the anagram below which is of three connected words. For example hop, skip, jump.

UNWARRANTED RUDE GHQ

Which bracketed word is most opposite in meaning to the key word?

IMBIBE   (reject, acquire, gather, imagine, portray)

From the following six words select the two which are opposite in meaning.

apprehend, dauntless, boorish, bargain, modest, civil

Add a letter to a word meaning bring about to create a small native range horse.

Complete the following palindrome by inserting the missing word/s:

Sums are not set as a test on *******

Take two of the three-letter elements and combine them to make a six-letter word which fits the keyword definition.

TREES (ALM, BRA, CHE, RRI, SIL, OND)

plate, rear, pipe, pale, daze

Change one letter in each word to find five new words on the same theme.

Place a word in the brackets that means the same as the definitions outside the brackets.

Bottom (   )   despicable

Place a word in the brackets that means the same as the definitions outside the brackets.

Narrow opening   (   )   sound of coins striking together

whale, kingdom, lunar, reign

which word below continues the above sequence?

rain, cloud, shower, thunder, wind

Danube   scolds   verify

Who comes next?

Evelyn, Pamela, Agatha, Sheila, Yvonne

What do these pairs of words have in common?

lemur	alcove		crock	yield
scalp	snake		stand	espy

Place a word in the brackets that means the same as the definitions outside the brackets.

Grasp (   )   storage area

Use every letter of the phrase CURES A WEAK SPLUTTER once each only to spell out three kitchen implements.

Add a letter to a firearm to produce a word meaning flick through the pages of a book.

What do the following words have in common?

salon, tier, money, sail

Add a letter to a word meaning afterward to produce a word meaning the second of two.

Place the same word in front of each of these words to make five new words.

```
( - - - - )        BALL
                   BATH
                   PAD
                   LOOSE
                   PATH
```

Change one letter of an animal shelter to produce a single seed.

Add a letter to a word meaning more coarse to produce a steering system.

Which 9-letter word contains the repeated letter sequence LALA?

* * L A L A * * *

If meat in a river (3 in 6) is T(HAM)ES can you find precipitation in a headache (4 in 8)?

Which two words that are anagrams of each other mean in speech, a type of preposition and nonchalant?

Solve the anagrams, which are all of numbers which increase in value, for example evens = seven.

Shirty event
Fix story
Nifty foe

What is an AXIOM?

(a)	Part of a ship	(c)	Self evident truth
(b)	Spindle	(d)	Group of trees

Select two words that are synonyms, plus an antonym of these two synonyms, from the following list.

oblivious, consuming, immoral, unaware, congenial, attentive, unpleasant

All the answers to the clues are two words. The two words in each answer both start with the same letter.

Cosmic explosion
Harmonious smoking implement
Pale yellowish grape juice
A body set up to find solutions to problems
Deadline
Natural gas and petroleum, for example
Woman of fortune

Change one letter only in each word below to form a familiar phrase.

BUD PAIR MAY

From the following six words select the two which are closest in meaning.

hallowed, annoy, dedicate, desist, revered, regular

COURT RALLY

Change one letter in each word above to produce two words similar in meaning.

Insert a word in the brackets so that it completes a word or phrase when tacked onto the word on the left and completes another word or phrase when placed in front of the word on the right.

Boots ( ) door

Start with a young animal (4 letters)
Change a letter to find a source of illumination
Change a letter to find a bivouac
Change a letter to produce moistness
Change a letter to find a lady
Change a letter to find a Scandinavian
Change a letter to find a thoroughfare
Change a letter to produce a straight row
Change a letter to find a fruit
Change a letter to describe a feeble excuse
Change a letter to obtain the same young animal you started out with

Famous Name Anagrams – who are the following?

a) 20th-century German politician, known as *der alte* or *the old man* (6,8)
   ROUND NAKED AREA

b) Operatic tenor who was given the nickname *the man with the orchid-lined voice* (6,6)
   RANCOROUS ICE

c) American Civil War general and indian fighter (6,9,6)
   CURSE STRONGER MORTGAGE

d) Italian-English author of novels such as *The Sea Hawk* (1915) and *Captain Blood* (1936) (6,8)
   A FATAL SIBERIAN

Solve the six clues to find three pairs of words that reverse their letters (palindromes), for example DEVIL – LIVED

Charts	Pressurised	Refunded
Junk mail	Sweets	Towel or napkin

Which bracketed word is most similar in meaning to the key word?

PATHETIC   (countenanced, composed, pitiable, helpful, excited)

When presented with the words am, mar and far and asked to find the shortest word in the English language from which these three words could be produced I would expect you to come up with the word FARM. Now here is a further set of words. Which is the shortest word in the English language from which these words can be produced?

MOUND   PONY   POSED

Which bracketed word is most similar in meaning to the key word?

DREGS   (potion, grounds, trail, outline, precise)

The object outside the brackets always has two of the features inside the brackets. Identify which two

Hexagon (six lines, six sides, eight sides, eight angles, 600º)

In the phrase below the first letter of each word has been removed as well as spacing. What is the phrase?

UTFTEP

When presented with the words am, mar and far and asked to find the shortest word in the English language from which these three words could be produced I would expect you to come up with the word FARM. Now here is a further set of words. Which is the shortest word in the English language from which these words can be produced?

CENSOR   NURSE   SOLD

What is the longest word that can be produced from the ten letters below? No letter may be used more than once.

EMPIGACLUF

Complete the hyphenated word below

* * * * * * * * O P – Q * * * * * *

CAL   CIT   CDE

Insert the same four-letter word into the letter arrangements above to produce three words.

Solve the anagram below which is of three connected words. For example hop, skip, jump.

ONE HORNLIKE SKI

Insert a word in the brackets so that it completes a word or phrase when tacked onto the word on the left and completes another word or phrase when placed in front of the word on the right.

Brain ( ) cloud

What commonality is shared by the words flash, sad, dash, flags, half, gash, ask and lad?

If meat in a river (3 in 6) is T(HAM)ES can you find a U.S. president in something reasonably priced (4 in 10)?

Solve the clues below. All the answers are a two word phrase, with only two letters in each word.

A sunken fence
Equipment for the reproduction of sound
Make over

If meat in a river (3 in 6) is T(HAM)ES can you find a fish in a reptile (3 in 9)?

Solve the four clues. The four answers can then be combined to produce two hyphenated words.

A mass of filaments growing from the skin of an animal
Large rapacious bird of the falcon family
Extend in length and breadth
A large ruminant

Take a punctuation mark, reverse it, and then add a letter at the front and another at the back to produce a type of bed. What is the punctuation mark and the type of bed?

What do the following words all have in common?
machination, formality, incubate, schadenfreude

Complete the following palindrome by inserting the missing word/s:

Nurse, I spy *******, run

CHANGE FRIAR is an anagram of which two words that when combined form an hyphenated phrase.

CASTLE   is to   keep as
DANCE HALL   is to   (foyer, band, dancing, music, entertainment)

From the following six words select the two which are opposite in meaning.

swamp, insult, forward, subside, bloom, nonplus

Insert two letters in each set of brackets so that they finish the word on the left and start the word on the right. The letters inserted when read downwards in pairs must spell out an eight-letter word.

LI (**) UD
BI (**) HY
GL (**) EX
MU (**) VY

Take two of the three-letter elements and combine them to make a six-letter word which fits the keyword definition.

ANIMALS   (CAT, COU, TLE, GER, HEI, FAR)

Insert a word in the brackets so that it completes a word or phrase when tacked onto the word on the left and completes another word or phrase when placed in front of the word on the right.

meadow   (   )   spur

Remove a letter from a word meaning *a bowl-shaped cavity* to leave a word meaning *to provide food*.

I have withdrawn my presence despite lacking the liberty granted which would remove the restraint from my actions. What is my current situation?

a. Change a bird to an animal by changing the first letter
b. Change one bird into a variety of birds by adding a letter to the front
c. Change the second letter of a bird to make a tree

If meat in a river (3 in 6) is T(HAM)ES can you find a relative in a leisurely stroll (4 in 7)?

MAN UTD SOARS is an anagram of which historical character born in 1503?

Place one of the fruits in the first column between one of the groups of letters in the second column until you have produced six words.

For example: GRD + APPLE = GR*APPLE*D

date   subly
peach   aped
lime   bng
pear   sed
ugli   efy
fig   imment

Change **MOUSE** to **HOLE** by producing compound words at each stage with the aid of the letters provided, for example: change BLACK to HOLE by proceeding black - mail - man - hole.

MOUSE
* * A *
* O * R
* T * *
* A * H * *
* * N *
* A * K
* * M *
* U *
* O *
HOLE

Place the same word in front of each of these words to make five new words.

(- - - - -)

FED
MINE
STAND
STOOD
RATED

Which word is the odd one out?

intoxicate, senator, madden, regiment, reaction, demand, observe, excitation, teach, creation, statement, verbose, treason, cheat, testament

From the following six words select the two which are closest in meaning.

cabal, visage, delight, reality, clique, artful

Find two of the three words: that can be paired to form an anagram that is a synonym of the remaining word. For example, with LEG - MEEK - NET, the words LEG and NET form an anagram of GENTLE, which is a synonym of the remaining word, MEEK.

Into – preface – inductor

Each of the following word combinations rhymes with a well-known phrase, for example *fight and play* rhymes with *night and day*.

Can you work out the phrases?

rock and scull   fat and log   rebut and begun

Each three-word phrase has been hidden by removing the initial letters of each word and then removing the space between them. For example *odds and ends* would become DDSNDNDS and *get the message* would become ETHEESSAGE

ATUMBLEIE   ONEHEISER   AKEOEART

What is a Bêch-de-Mer?

(a)	Seaweed	(c)	Coral
(b)	Rich sauce	(d)	Sea cucumber

Test Eight: Question 31

All the vowels have been removed from this trite saying and the remaining consonants split into four groups of eight. What is the saying? All the consonants remain in the same order.

THDFFCLT   SSYNDTHM   PSSBLSLT   TLBTHRDR

Test Eight: Question 32

Invented in 1879 by Lewis Carroll, the puzzle which he named *Doublets* but which is now probably better known as *Word Ladders*, consists of proposing two words of the same length and converting one word into the other by changing one letter at a time and forming new words at each stage. The new words formed are called links, for example change HEAD into TAIL in four links: solution HEAD - HEAL - TEAL - TELL - TALL - TAIL; heal, teal, tell and tall being the four links.

Now try the following:

Change PIG to STY in 4 links

Test Eight: Question 33

Find three trees hidden in the following two sentences:

I strode out quickly over the firm ground.
The clothes were soaking in the wash tub.

Test Eight: Question 34

Arrange the letters of each word below to find three words which all begin with the letters AM

LIBYA
NAOMI
TONGS

Which bracketed word is most similar in meaning to the key word?

INDISCREET   (rash, furious, neutral, insulting, slight)

Which two words that are anagrams of each other mean afraid and relating to religion?

SIDE   QUICK   BRAND
                ?
                CROSS

What word is missing?

Which two words that are anagrams of each other mean damsel and the middle value?

When presented with the words am, mar and far and asked to find the shortest word in the English language from which these three words could be produced I would expect you to come up with the word FARM. Now here is a further set of words. Which is the shortest word in the English language from which these words can be produced?

CRASH   APRIL   CHAPEL

If meat in a river (3 in 6) is T(HAM)ES can you find a middle eastern country in a dangerous fish (4 in 7)?

The answer to the following clues is a pair of rhyming words, for example, unhappy young man = sad lad

pull floor covering

Solve the following line by line to produce an eight-letter word:

My first is in Christmas but not in cracker,
My second's in computer but not in hacker,
My third is in animal but not in bird,
My fourth is in fourth but not in third,
My fifth is in morning but not in night,
My sixth is in aeroplane but not in flight,
My seventh's in original but not in thing,
My eighth's in winter but never spring,
Look forward to living each new day,
For the answer to this won't go away.

What phrase (3, 4, 8, 3, 5, 4) is indicated by the arrangement of letters below?

STEPPETSPETS

A well-known phrase has had all its vowels removed and has been split into groups of three letters. What is the phrase?

All remaining letters are in the same order.

FRB   TTR   RFR   WRS

Complete the seven words, each of which contains the word SIN, with the aid of the clues.

SIN******	genuine or honestly
*SIN*****	mica
SIN**	destroy germs
SIN	unsteadiness as a result of alcohol
****SIN**	thanks-givings
*****SIN*	large luxurious sedan
******SIN	State of the US

The object outside the brackets always has two of the features inside the brackets. Identify which two

Chess (rook, clock, onlooker, passed pawn, bishop)

Arrange these eighteen 3-letter words into six groups so that each group spells out a 9-letter word.

try	eve	one	ran
ill	pen	pan	red
woe	tor	lop	tag
ten	beg	ram	man
war	got		

Solve the anagrams below to find five words which all have a common theme.

her BBC cameo
cure TV magician
eighth soul
new stardom
cut red runner

Which is the odd one out?

The American Dream
The Grand Canyon
A Little Englander
The Prodigal Son
A Neanderthal Man
The Ten Commandments

The answer to the following clues is a pair of rhyming words, for example, unhappy young man = sad lad

trading a residence

Solve the anagrams of four words below which are all similar in meaning:

Spindled
A mild bear
Make barrel
Bum lies

Solve the anagram below which is of three connected words. For example hop, skip, jump.

BLOCK NOBLE DEAL

Solve the cryptic clue below. The answer is an anagram contained within the clue:

Repair tiny article elaborately

Find a reason for combining the words below into four pairs:

nib, nod, rent, raw, go, rant, rot, par

Of the following five words, four have a common theme. Which is the odd one out?

hyena, koala, dottrel, coney, lynx

You are looking for a one-word answer to this riddle:

You cannot see me, but watch what I do,
Many a function I provide for you,
Some people like me, some do not,
I've been around since time forgot,
Look for directions in part of me,
The lucky part is that I'm free,
Find me, you're nearly there,
I can be most anywhere.

Use the letters of the phrase AN ANT HARASSED ANIMALS once each only to spell out three girl's names which all begin with the same letter.

Solve the clue below to find a pair of words.

    P L * * *   * * * * A Y

Aircraft SOS

aquatic	Quoits
earwig	Upset
?	Visible
Mikado	Great

What word is missing?

Hilarious, interim, ink, hair, harm

Find a tree in each of the following sentences

Grandmother always used to boil the tea kettle whenever we went to visit.
The battalion was ordered to slope arms prior to inspection.
Named for the Roman god of war, Mars is also sometimes referred to as the red planet.

From the following six words select the two which are opposite in meaning.

fidgety, dreamy, cruel, flaming, practical, falsehood

Complete the hyphenated word below.

* * * N – O P * * * * * *

Take two of the three-letter elements and combine them to make a six-letter word which fits the keyword definition.

VEGETABLES   (MAR, POT, RAD, ICH, OTA, ROW)

Place a word in the brackets that means the same as the definitions outside the brackets.

Stony   (   )   unsteady

Complete the hyphenated word below

* * * S S – S * * * * * *

Complete the following palindrome by inserting the missing word/s:

Sir, I demand, I am a **** named Iris

The three clues refer to a synonym, an antonym and an anagram (*in no particular order*). Figure out the answer word in each case. For example: halt, post, start; Answer word: stop; Post (anagram), halt (synonym), start (antonym)

learning, illiteracy, cautioned
mental, rejoice, bewail
abundance, thread, insufficiency

| LOS ANGELES | is to | California as |
| LAS VEGAS | is to | (Maryland, Nebraska, Nevada, Wyoming, Ohio) |

Each of the following word combinations rhymes with a well-known phrase, for example *fight and play* rhymes with *night and day*. Can you work out the phrases?

chew and fry   stun and dames   then and stink

Solve the clues below. All the answers are a two word phrase, with only two letters in each word.

Neither very good nor very bad
Commotion
Type of toy

Change one letter only in each word below *and then change the order of the words* to form a familiar phrase.

KEG AID LACK UDDER

SHY   HST   SH

Insert three 3-letter words into the middle of the letter arrangements to produce three 6-letter words. The three 3-letter words inserted must form a familiar phrase.

Place the same word in front of each of these words to make five new words.

        (- - -)   SON
                               BOIL
                               DON
                               TAKE
                               RED

If meat in a river (3 in 6) is T(HAM)ES can you find a rodent in charity (4 in 11)?

What three-letter word can be placed in front of the letters below to create five four-letter words?

T
Y
P
E
D

Find two of the three words: that can be paired to form an anagram that is a synonym of the remaining word. For example, with LEG - MEEK - NET, the words LEG and NET form an anagram of GENTLE, which is a synonym of the remaining word, MEEK.

Din – mean – impound

Insert the name of a creature into the bottom line to complete the 3-letter words reading downwards:

T	P	G	S	W	S	M	D	F
E	A	E	K	A	E	A	U	I
*	*	*	*	*	*	*	*	*

Each of the following is an anagram of a profession or occupation.

notice priest
Cyril Baker
linked name

From the following six words select the two which are closest in meaning.

figment, faculty, rebellion, sedition, capacity, terminal

What do the following all have in common?

Sally, Sam, goose, time, knot, clock

What is EUCHRE?

(a)   Poisonous drink
(b)   Fancy shirt
(c)   Type of knife
(d)   Card game

The answer to the following clues is a pair of rhyming words, for example, unhappy young man = sad lad

less speedy grass cutter

Add four consecutive letters of the alphabet, not necessarily in the correct order to complete the word below.

* * * I * A T E

Which four bits can be joined together to produce two words that have opposite meanings?

ely, mir, ees, pid, ton, liv, ear, tor, sil, one

EEEELNN

Add the same letter six times to the above group of letters and then rearrange the thirteen resultant letters to produce a thirteen-letter word meaning inanity.

Solve the anagrams below which all contain the letters C A S E, for example CASE + BEN = absence

CASE + TRAIN =
CASE + EDICT =
CASE + DINER =

Each three-word phrase has been hidden by removing the initial letters of each word and then removing the space between them.

For example *odds and ends* would become DDSNDNDS and *get the message* would become ETHEESSAGE

ARNDEACE   TONGAST   NOODHAPE

Remove a letter from a lithograph to leave a liquid measure.

The object outside the brackets always has two of the features inside the brackets. Identify which two

Train (wheels, restaurant car, ticket inspector, rails, bridge)

Change a pair of double letters in a word meaning milliner to another pair of double letters to produce a type of hand tool.

Add four consecutive letters of the alphabet, not necessarily in the correct order to complete the word below.

C * * * A * D

Which four bits can be joined together to produce two words that have similar meanings?

oun, row, may, bea, plo, fur, can, oun, ugh, iph

AELU

Add the same letter three times to the above group of letters and then rearrange the seven resultant letters to produce a seven-letter word meaning cases.

Change a pair of double letters in a word meaning a light two-wheeled vehicle to another pair of double letters to produce a word meaning crony.

Invented in 1879 by Lewis Carroll, the puzzle which he named *Doublets* but which is now probably better known as *Word Ladders*, consists of proposing two words of the same length and converting one word into the other by changing one letter at a time and forming new words at each stage. The new words formed are called links, for example change HEAD into TAIL in four links: solution HEAD - HEAL - TEAL - TELL - TALL - TAIL; heal, teal, tell and tall being the four links.
Now try the following:

Change HAND to FOOT in 5 links

Use every letter of the phrase POOL LOYAL INFANTS once each only to spell out three types of horse.

The clue spacious heath leads to which pair of words that are palindromic (for example erupt pure)

Remove a letter from a word meaning husky to leave a hoofed quadruped.

Complete the words which all mean GREAT. Then rearrange the first letter of each to find another word meaning GREAT.

* A * T
* B * N * A * T
* I * N * F * C * N *
* A * M * T *
* U * E * I * R
* N * R * O * S
I * M * N * E

Solve the anagrams, the number of letters is indicated, to complete a quotation.

```
* *   * * *   * * /  * * * * *    * * / * * * * * * *    * * * * * *
```
rioters (2,3,2)   thou man   (5,2)   go refine vivid (7,6)

Which bracketed word is most opposite in meaning to the key word?

DERIDE   (ridicule, gibe, taunt, respect, specify)

Insert a word in the brackets so that it completes a word or phrase when tacked onto the word on the left and completes another word or phrase when placed in front of the word on the right.

grease   (   )   brush

E   L   N   O   ?   N   L   D   A   O   N   N   D

What letter should replace the question mark?

Which bracketed word is most opposite in meaning to the key word?

MACABRE   (charming, ghastly, horrid, cunning, intriguing)

Solve the anagram below which is of three connected words. For example hop, skip, jump.

GRAB A BIG TOTAL

Find two of the three words: that can be paired to form an anagram that is a synonym of the remaining word. For example, with LEG - MEEK - NET, the words LEG and NET form an anagram of GENTLE, which is a synonym of the remaining word, MEEK.

criterion – sun – revolt

If 9L of a C is nine lives of a cat, can you decode the following?   81 S in a S P

FREE SCATTY TIT is an anagram of which two words that are similar in meaning?

Complete the following palindrome by inserting the missing word/s:

Kay, a red nude ****** under a yak

From the following six words select the two which are opposite in meaning.

inspire, impulse, doctrine, coach, custom, dishearten

The phrase below has had its initial letters and word boundaries removed. What is the phrase?

HEEAROT

Insert three 3-letter words into the middle of the letter arrangements to produce three words. The three 3-letter words inserted must form a familiar phrase.

STLE   BIT   CCH

Of the following five words, four have a common theme. Which is the odd one out?

pate, pork, sherry, rice, jelly

The clue *loose lifting device* leads to which pair of rhyming words?

Change one letter only in each word to form a familiar phrase.   ART   FOUR   ACE

Take two of the three-letter elements and combine them to make a six-letter word which fits the keyword definition.

CRIME   (FOR, PAR, PRI, SIN, DEN, GER)

What phrase is indicated below?

C H # .

When presented with the words am, mar and far and asked to find the shortest word in the English language from which these three words could be produced I would expect you to come up with the word FARM. Now here is a further set of words. Which is the shortest word in the English language from which these words can be produced?

PIRATE   MAZE   AZURE

Each of the following word combinations rhymes with a well-known phrase, for example *fight and play* rhymes with *night and day*. Can you work out the phrases?

cup and crown   feeling and ceiling   madam and relieve

From the following six words select the two which are closest in meaning.

entangle, glib, standstill, slippery, blunder, habit

CON   GEN   SER

Insert three 3-letter words into the middle of the letter arrangements to produce three 6-letter words. The three 3-letter words inserted must form a familiar phrase.

Complete the hyphenated phrase below.

* * * TY – F I * * *

Test Ten: Question 23

Each of the following is an anagram of a profession or occupation.

train music   runs to jail   weird return

Test Ten: Question 24

The answer to the following clues is a pair of rhyming words, for example, unhappy young man = sad lad

more elevated singing group

Test Ten: Question 25

Each three-word phrase has been hidden by removing the initial letters of each word and then removing the space between them. For example *odds and ends* would become DDSNDNDS and *get the message* would become ETHEESSAGE

ALLNTOLACE   OREATHAKES   EVENEARTCH

Test Ten: Question 26

Place the same word in front of each of these words to make five new words.

       (- - - -)   RATE
                              FLOW
                              STATE
                              ACT
                              LAY

Test Ten: Question 27

APPLE   is to   fruit as
FIR   is to   (tree, wood, bush, branches, twigs)

Solve the anagrams, the number of letters is indicated, to complete a quotation.

* * *   * * * *   /   * * * * *   * * * * * * *   /   * * *   * * * * *

eke them (3,4)   hellish train (5,7)   three hat (3,5)

Change one letter only in each word below to form a familiar phrase.

BUT I BRAKE FAME OF AT

Use each letter of the phrase PORKIER DERISIBLE GOAT once each only to spell out three card games.

What is a BROCK?

- (a)   Type of cup
- (b)   Store tower
- (c)   Badger
- (d)   Compressed coal dust

Select two words that are synonyms, plus an antonym of these two synonyms, from the list of words below.

clarify, irritate, soothe, treat, elucidate, cure, pacify

Solve the anagrams below. Every answer contains the letters S O L V E.

For example SOLVE + IT = VIOLETS

SOLVE + PERT =
SOLVE + RUIN =
SOLVE + ICES =
SOLVE + BLAIN =
SOLVE + LINES =

Add four consecutive letters of the alphabet, not necessarily in the correct order to complete the word below.

* O L D * * S *

Due to the ravages of time, situations or circumstances, I am inferior in condition to that which I was previously. What is my current condition?

Change one letter only in each word below to form a familiar phrase.

ROD SANE TIE RING

Of the following five words, four have a common theme. Which is the odd one out?

topaz, ruby, doily, garnet, pearl

Which bracketed word is most similar in meaning to the key word?

FACTION   (edifice, border, cover, clique, veneer)

Complete the hyphenated word below:

* * U R T – M A * * * * *

The object outside the brackets always has two of the features inside the brackets. Identify which two

Horse (coat, stable, hair, teeth, paddock)

The answer to the following clues is a pair of rhyming words, for example, unhappy young man = sad lad

gloomy recreation area

Place a word in the brackets that means the same as the definitions outside the brackets.

Journal   (   )   arsenal

What do the following all have in common?

saunas, lamina, quoit, hasten

Complete the words below which are all similar in meaning. The first letter of each spells out another word of similar meaning.

```
* P * C * A * U * A *
* N * E * I * V * B * E
* H * N * M * N * L
* X * E * L * N *
* E * A * K * B * E
* R * A * H * A * I * G
```

Invented in 1879 by Lewis Carroll, the puzzle which he named *Doublets* but which is now probably better known as *Word Ladders*, consists of proposing two words of the same length and converting one word into the other by changing one letter at a time and forming new words at each stage. The new words formed are called links, for example change HEAD into TAIL in four links: solution HEAD - HEAL - TEAL - TELL - TALL - TAIL; heal, teal, tell and tall being the four links. Now try the following:

Change MORE to LESS in 3 links

TWIST ZOO DUNCE and GOT ONE AWKWARD POET are both anagrams of which two phrases (3, 4, 2, 4 and 4, 4, 1, 3, 2, 3) which are very similar in meaning?
Clue: to humble

What do the following all have in common?

Strategic defence initiative
Film noir
Genus thamnophilus
Designer stubble

The clue heavenly group of singers leads to which pair of rhyming words?

I am making a sound which usually emanates from a quadruped of the genus Canus in the direction of the more elevated position of a misguided woody plant of considerable size. What am I doing?

Which bracketed word is most similar in meaning to the key word?

FACTIOUS   (unnatural, malcontent, rebellious, turbulent, unnatural)

Of the following five words, four have a common theme. Which is the odd one out?

sabre, sword, musket, rapier, dagger

Complete the names below of worldwide towns and cities, only alternate letters are given. Then rearrange the initial letters of each into another city.

* O * O * T *
* S * E * D
* I * D * O * E *
* V * G * O *

* A * R * S
* A * A * A * I
* I * E * I * K
* O * T * R * A *

BIS   APEE

Insert two 5-letter words into the middle of the letter arrangements to produce two words. The two 5-letter words inserted must form a familiar phrase.

SIY   AFD   GEN

Insert three 3-letter words into the middle of the letter arrangements to produce three words. The three 3 – letter words inserted must form a familiar phrase.

Remove a letter from a word meaning squirm to leave a word meaning correspond.

Solve the clues to find four six-letter words. The same three letters are represented by XYZ in each word.

XYZ***	member of the legal profession
*XYZ**	scratched with nail
**XYZ*	African country
***XYZ	lawbreaker

Find a seasonal phrase of two words (6, 10) in which each of the two words start with a 3-letter word as indicated by the asterisks. The second of these 3-letter words is the past participle of the first of the 3-letter words.

* * *
_ _ _ 　　　* * *
_ _ _ _ _ _ _

Each of the following word combinations rhymes with a well-known phrase, for example *fight and play* rhymes with *night and day*. Can you work out the phrases?

cigars and pipes　　　sigh and charge　　　flat and dowse

| BRIGAND | is to | robber as a |
| FARRIER | is to | (herdsman, shoesmith, shearer, vendor, coster) |

Combine three of the three letter bits to produce a word meaning engage in plotting.

tap　　ale　　hin　　are　　mac　　ere　　ise　　ate　　ole

Remove a letter from a word meaning pillager to leave a word meaning an appended clause.

From the following six words select the two which are opposite in meaning.

inviolate, unstained, obligatory, animate, habitual, corrupt

Solve the anagrams, the number of letters is indicated, to complete a quotation.

*** *** ** / ******** **** / *** *****

tin sheep (3,3, 2)   hit nightmare (8,4)   two herds (3,5)

Take two of the three-letter elements and combine them to make a six-letter word which fits the keyword definition.

ART   (STA, MOS, AIC, TUW, STU, DII)

Each of the following is an anagram of a profession or occupation.

shooting patrol
brain lair
USA dog cart
stoic outline

Select two words that are synonyms, plus an antonym of these two synonyms, from the list of words below.

intense, erudite, notable, learned, illiterate, fundamental, strong

Complete the words below so that the same two letters that finish the first word start the second word and the same two letters that finish the second word start the third word etc. The same two letters that finish the sixth word also start the first word to complete the circle.

```
** DU **
** MO **
** AC **
** BE **
** TA **
** OS **
```

Find two of the three words: that can be paired to form an anagram that is a synonym of the remaining word. For example, with LEG - MEEK - NET, the words LEG and NET form an anagram of GENTLE, which is a synonym of the remaining word, MEEK.

Elite – rescue – bar

CUD   MUD   UPT   DAD

What four-letter word can be inserted into the letter arrangements above to form four words?

Solve the anagram below which is of three connected words. For example hop, skip, jump.

LETHAL SOLAR TREK

Complete the following palindrome by inserting the missing word/s:

Doc, note, I dissent, a fast never prevents a *******, I diet on cod.

FART UPON RISING is an anagram of which two words that are opposite in meaning?

Make ICE into SKATER by following these instructions and producing good English words at each stage.

		ICE
i.	change a letter	***
ii.	change a letter	***
iii.	add three letters	SKATER

The answer to the following clues is a pair of rhyming words, for example, unhappy young man = sad lad

high spirited parrot

Place the same word in front of each of these words to make five new words.

```
( - - - - - )            DOG
                         STAND
                         STATE
                         ESTIMATE
                         LING
```

Test Eleven: **Question 26**

Select two words that are synonyms, plus an antonym of these two synonyms, from the list of words below.

recruit, reform, dismiss, contact, waylay, enrol, promote

Test Eleven: **Question 27**

From the following six words select the two which are closest in meaning.

insatiable, deranged, indiscreet, innocent, rapacious, unkind

---

Test Eleven: **Question 28**

ADORES WORDS is an anagram of which two words that sound alike but are spelled differently and have different meanings?

Test Eleven: **Question 29**

Add four consecutive letters of the alphabet, not necessarily in the correct order to complete the word below.

* L O R I * I * *

Test Eleven: **Question 30**

The clue *gain additional points* leads to which pair of rhyming words?

If meat in a river (3 in 6) is T(HAM)ES can you find a pop group in a vegetable (4 in 7)?

What is a CAMPANILE?

    (a)   Musical theme
    (b)   Type of bird
    (c)   Bell tower
    (d)   Stately dance

Which bracketed word is most opposite in meaning to the key word?

INDIRECT   (circuitous, manifest, straight, unsettled, confused)

Which two words that are spelled differently but are pronounced the same mean particle and power?

Below are seven forms of transportation. Take one letter from each in turn to spell out another form of transportation.

streetcar, truck, taxi, cycle, jet, coach, train

The clue football pop star leads to which pair of rhyming words?

Which two words that are spelled the same but pronounced differently mean access and enchant?

Find a capital city and a type of deciduous tree. Both are the same number of letters long and have the same number of consonants which appear in the same position and same order in both names.

The object outside the brackets always has two of the features inside the brackets. Identify which two

Ferry (boat, wheel, sailor, passengers, sail)

Insert a word in the brackets so that it completes a word or phrase when tacked onto the word on the left and completes another word or phrase when placed in front of the word on the right.

    Wind ( )   dream

When presented with am, mar and far and asked to find the shortest word in the English language from which these three words could be produced I would expect you to come up with the word FARM. Now here is a further set of words. Which is the shortest word in the English language from which these words can be produced?
    CRYPT   BARN   UNPACK

Use every letter of the phrase DETECT BEER BEARER once each only to spell out three words meaning to move back.

Combine four of the three-letter bits to produce two words that are similar in meaning.

man, tap, ugh, ect, ipt, ack, asp, ner, int, ere

Which bracketed word is most opposite in meaning to the key word?

HALLOWED   (consecrate, blessed, dedicated, desecrated, revered)

The answer to the following clues is a pair of rhyming words, for example, unhappy young man = sad lad

clutch a lash

What is the meaning of MACHIAVELLIAN?

a. evil   d. scheming
b. dangerous   e. arrogant
c. fiendish

Insert two letters in each set of brackets so that they complete the word on the left and start the word on the right. The letters inserted must spell out an eight-letter word when read downwards in pairs.

        JU (**) LL
        FA (**) IR
        GO (**) OM
        DO (**) AL

Use every letter of the phrase CUTE SLAVE GIRL RIOTS once each only to spell out three words meaning an invitee.

Change one letter only in each word below to form a familiar phrase.

IN ARE IS SHE HOME

Which of the following is not an anagram of a type of cheese?

CRAB MET ME
LOAM RAZZLE
SMEAR PAN
FLOG RANDY

drum
ragtime
medley
flautist

?
legato
trumpet
duet

From the choice below, which is the missing word?

Kettle, soprano, fanfare, band, piano, violinist

Solve the following enclosure:

For example: stardom in a country (4 in 6,6,2,7)
Answer: United States o(**f Ame**)rica

wildebeeste in a bottle of champagne (3 in 6)

In each of the following replace two of the words or phrases in the sentence with two heteronyms without changing the meaning of the sentence, for example:
The burden was our responsibility. Answer: The onus was on us.

I moved the large book in my direction

What is the longest word that can be produced from each of the two words below. Letters can only be used once each only in each word. For example, the longest word that can be produced using the letters of the word INTERJECT no more than once each only is RETICENT.

AUTHORITY
BANDWAGON

Of the following five words, four have a common theme. Which is the odd one out?

ling, cod, minnow, basset, plaice

Find the abbreviation, for example 9 L of a C = 9 lives of a cat

0 D L of the E

The letters of the two countries BELARUS / INDIA can be arranged to spell out the names of two other countries. Can you find them? All twelve letters must be used once each only.

A Kangaroo word is a word which carries within it a smaller word which is a synonym e.g. destruction - ruin. All letters of the smaller word have to be in the correct order, but not necessarily adjacent. Find the Kangaroo Words contained in the words below:

blossoms, calumnies

Solve the anagram below which is of three connected names. For example TORY CHARM KID is an anagram of Tom, Dick, Harry.

PATRIOTS MASS, HOORAH!

Which bracketed word is most similar in meaning to the key word?

FETTER   (manacle, artisan, robust, hackle, limp)

Solve the clue below to find a pair of words.

    P L * * *   * * * * * A Y

Lavish exhibition

From the following six words select the two which are opposite in meaning.

seniority, malice, colossal, employee, goodwill, superintend

Take two of the three-letter elements and combine them to make a six-letter word which fits the keyword definition.

WEATHER   (CLO, SHO, WIR, SQU, ILL, UDY)

The answer to the following clues is a pair of rhyming words, for example, unhappy young man = sad lad

call for return to custody

cast, able, icon, edit, neck, ?

What comes next?

barn, talk, take, afar, more, coin

Solve the cryptic clue below. The answer is an anagram contained within the clue:

Jive around with cadet when in descriptive mood.

In each case, change one letter only from each word to produce a familiar phrase. For example; *plan in works* would become *play on words*.

some clear
to on did

If meat in a river (3 in 6) is T(HAM)ES can you find a lepidopterous insect in a book of the New Testament (4 in 7)?

Solve the following enclosure: For example: stardom in a country (4 in 6,6,2,7)
            Answer: United States o(**f Ame**)rica

organ of smell in a very brief moment of time (4 in 10)

Add five consecutive letters of the alphabet, not necessarily in the correct order to complete the word below.

RRI*A

The clues *rapscallion* and *part of a church* lead to which pair of words that sound alike but are spelled differently?

Which three-letter word, when placed in the brackets, completes the first word and starts the second?

HAT   (***)   DEN

Add four consecutive letters of the alphabet and then rearrange the ten resultant letters to produce a ten-letter word meaning charming.

DILLTU

Place the same word in front of each of these words to make five new words.

        (----)   LIGHT
                      BEAM
                      SHINE
                      GLOW
                      RAKER

Which four bits can be joined together to produce two words that have opposite meanings?

ast, eer, pur, lon, ify, wil, oul, all, ore, bef

What do the following words have in common?

HOP   BET
MAR   TIN
RUB   HAZE

What is a CARBOY?

      (a)   Wicker covered bottle
      (b)   Revolving barrel
      (c)   Pungent plant
      (d)   Servant

Complete the following palindrome by inserting the missing word/s:

'Tis **** on a visit

Add four consecutive letters of the alphabet, not necessarily in the correct order to complete the word below.

                              * L O R I * I * *

Test Twelve: Question 30

The answer to the following clues is a pair of rhyming words, for example, unhappy young man = sad lad

ancient precious metal

Test Twelve: Question 31

The object outside the brackets always has two of the features inside the brackets. Identify which two

Sofa (cushions, people, legs, upholstery, runners)

Test Twelve: Question 32

Find the abbreviation, for example 9 L of a C = 9 lives of a cat

5 R on the O F

Test Twelve: Question 33

A Kangaroo word is a word which carries within it a smaller word which is a synonym e.g. destruction - ruin. All letters of the smaller word have to be in the
correct order, but not necessarily adjacent. Find the Kangaroo Words contained in the words below:

catacomb   container   curtail

Test Twelve: Question 34

If meat in a river (3 in 6) is T(HAM)ES can you find a U.S. president in something reasonably priced (4 in 10)?

Test Twelve: Question 35

TWEAK SAD CRABS is an anagram of which two words that are opposite in meaning?

What other country can be paired with TONGA so that they can then be arranged to spell out two more country names?

Of the following five words, four have a common theme. Which is the odd one out?

dingo, cairn, barbet, borzoi, lorikeet

Insert a word in the brackets so that it completes a word or phrase when tacked onto the word on the left and completes another word or phrase when placed in front of the word on the right.

Post   (   )   group

Solve the following enclosure: For example: stardom in a country (4 in 6,6,2,7)
        Answer: United States o(**f Ame**)rica

lion in a sailing ship (3 in 7)

The answer to the clue is a palindrome, e.g. uppermost container = top pot.

cared for open framework

If meat in a river (3 in 6) is T(HAM)ES can you find a middle eastern country in a dangerous fish (4 in 7)?

From the following six words select the two which are closest in meaning.

operate, continue, complicate, exhibition, pretext, perform

Find the abbreviation, for example 9 L of a C = 9 lives of a cat

9 P in the S S

Place a word in the brackets that means the same as the definitions outside the brackets.

Spick and span   (   )   type of tree

The following is an anagram of a palindromic phrase:

Soviet rioters (4, 2, 4, 3)

flat as a pancake
apples and pairs
anything goes

What comes next?

chalk and cheese   bean sprouts   intelligence test   work shy

The words *best* and *worst* are opposite in meaning. Can you find two more words that are opposite in meaning so that the first of these words rhymes with *best* and the second rhymes with *worst*?

Solve the cryptic clue below. The answer is an anagram contained within the clue:

Reconstructed neater column with descriptive appellation.

The answer to the following clues is a pair of rhyming words, for example, unhappy young man = sad lad

question intensely Shakespeare

A Kangaroo word is a word which carries within it a smaller word which is a synonym e.g. destruction - ruin. All letters of the smaller word have to be in the
correct order, but not necessarily adjacent. Find the Kangaroo Words contained in the words below:

deceased
deliberate
encourage

What should be the missing letters?

a R A   b. L E   e. Y E   f. U L
c. A N   d. L E   g. O P   h. ? ?

ER   US   HOR

Which four-letter word can precede all the above to produce three words.

In the phrase below the first letter of each word has been removed as well as spacing. What is the phrase?

ETSRAY

NEWR   BADMN   BALLER

Insert three 4-letter words into the middle of the letter arrangements to produce three words. The three 4-letter words inserted must form a familiar phrase.

Change numbers to letters to produce five eight-letter words that are all anagrams of each other.

```
1 2 3 4 5 6 7 8
5 4 2 1 3 6 7 8
3 5 6 1 7 8 2 4
1 2 4 5 3 6 7 8
6 7 3 4 8 5 1 2
```

When presented with the words am, mar and far and asked to find the shortest word in the English language from which these three words could be produced I would expect you to come up with the word FARM. Now here is a further set of words. Which is the shortest word in the English language from which these words can be produced?

EROTIC   MOAN   ROMP

Solve the following enclosure: For example: stardom in a country (4 in 6,6,2,7)
       Answer: United States o(**f Ame**)rica

kitchen appliance in a binding agreement (4 in 8)

LT   FILT   TESS

Insert the same four-letter word into the letter arrangements above to produce three words

Which bracketed word is most opposite in meaning to the key word?

GORGE   (devour, gent, gobble, starve, satiate)

Solve the anagram below which is of three connected names. For example TORY CHARM KID is an anagram of Tom, Dick, Harry.

CASH CHARMS BONEHEADED HAG

Test Thirteen: Question 11

From the following six words select the two which are opposite in meaning.

neglect, immolate, odorous, malodorous, chance, perform

Test Thirteen: Question 12

The answer to the following clues is a pair of rhyming words, for example, unhappy young man = sad lad

Atlantic movement

Test Thirteen: Question 13

If meat in a river (3 in 6) is T(HAM)ES can you find a coin in an alluvial deposit (4 in 8)?

Test Thirteen: Question 14

Of the following five words, four have a common theme. Which is the odd one out?

semi-circle, pentagon, sphere, circle, octagon

Test Thirteen: Question 15

If meat in a river (3 in 6) is T(HAM)ES can you find a Roman emperor in a barometer (4 in 7)?

Test Thirteen: Question 16

Take two of the three-letter elements and combine them to make a six-letter word which fits the keyword definition.

CITIES   (BER, LON, BOS, TIN, DOM, LIN)

Select two words that are synonyms, plus an antonym of these two synonyms, from the list of words below.

extreme, composed, contrived, quiet, agitated, confused, serene

What phrase is coded below?

KAMAHEETSOLSYLW

Insert the letters:

    AAAAACDGIINOOP

into the following once only to complete the palindrome:

* **G ! A **N** ** * P***D*

Which bracketed word is most opposite in meaning to the key word?

LIMPID   (clear, flexible, boundless, pellucid, opaque)

Add five consecutive letters of the alphabet, not necessarily in the correct order to complete the word below.

C * * * * A I *

Only one group of six letters below can be arranged to spell out a six-letter word in the English language. Find the word.

FUELNI   EBPOLY   ACTIPE
OEFLCI   NEFOGA
TILAEN   ANCUTY

In each of the following replace two of the words or phrases in the sentence with two heteronyms without changing the meaning of the sentence, for example:

The burden was our responsibility. Answer: The onus was on us.

It was the time of the year for the naval boy

From the following six words select the two which are closest in meaning.

frivolous, serene, distasteful, repulsive, shallow, adjust

Solve the following enclosure: For example: stardom in a country (4 in 6,6,2,7)
    Answer: United States o(**f Ame**)rica

musical instruments in a top marksperson (5 in 5,7)

Place the same word in front of each of these words to make five new words.

(- - - -)   LIGHT
                   LING
                   RING
                   TING
                   DUST

Test Thirteen: Question 27

The answer to the following clues is a pair of rhyming words, for example, unhappy young man = sad lad

clinking metallic sound

Test Thirteen: Question 28

What is a CAPYBARA?

      (a)   Tail-less rodent
      (b)   Eastern tree
      (c)   Muffler
      (d)   Coin

Test Thirteen: Question 29

```
*       *       *       *       *       *
U       O       R       O       N       E
N       T       I       O       C       W
*       *       *       *       *       *
```

Insert the names of two rivers, one on the top line and one on the bottom line to produce six four-letter words reading downwards.

Test Thirteen: Question 30

Find the abbreviation, for example 9 L of a C = 9 lives of a cat

17 S in a H

What is the longest word that can be produced from each of the two words below. Letters can only be used once each only in each word.

For example, the longest word that can be produced using the letters of the word INTERJECT no more than once each only is RETICENT.

CONUNDRUM
DIPLOMACY

The following is an anagram of a palindromic phrase:

comrades acted stormy (4, 6, 9)

A Kangaroo word is a word which carries within it a smaller word which is a synonym e.g. destruction - ruin. All letters of the smaller word have to be in the
correct order, but not necessarily adjacent. Find the Kangaroo Words contained in the words below:

evacuate   exists   fabrication

The answer to the clue is a palindrome, e.g. uppermost container = top pot.

choicest location

What other country can be paired with MALI so that they can be arranged to spell out two other country names?

Below are eight synonyms of the word SOUND. Find a further synonym of the word SOUND by taking one letter in turn from each of the eight synonyms. All letters are in the correct order.

noise, healthy, intact, wholesome, firm, stable, rational, well

What word is suggested by the group of words: Pascal, Coulomb, Kelvin?

The object outside the brackets always has two of the features inside the brackets. Identify which two

Soccer (goal posts, players, pitch, football, spectators)

Which bracketed word is most similar in meaning to the key word?

PATIENCE   (calmness, excitement, pitiable, tender, favoured)

Solve the clue, Lupine beast in assembly, to find a pair of words.
W O * * * * R D

Solve the following enclosure: For example: stardom in a country (4 in 6,6,2,7)
Answer: United States o(**f Ame**)rica

Roman Emperor in charitable (4 in 8)

Which bracketed word is most opposite in meaning to the key word?

NORM   (abnormal, pattern, standard, cool, peculiar)

In each of the following replace two of the words or phrases in the sentence with two heteronyms without changing the meaning of the sentence, for example: The burden was our responsibility. Answer: The onus was on us.

The staff were coping with the male's advancing years

The answer to the following clues is a pair of rhyming words, for example, unhappy young man = sad lad

astute stripper

Below are eight synonyms of the word HEROIC. Find a further synonym of the word HEROIC by taking one letter in turn from each of the six synonyms. All letters are in the correct order.

valiant, dauntless, stout, fearless, brave, plucky, audacious, bold

What does the following represent?

GNIKOOL
1875
1922
1972

Test Thirteen: Question 47

In each case, change one letter only from each word to produce a familiar phrase. For example; *plan in works* would become *play on words*.

sit on moss
all as case

Test Thirteen: Question 48

Find the abbreviation, for example 9 L of a C = 9 lives of a cat

20 Y S by R V W

Test Thirteen: Question 49

A Kangaroo word is a word which carries within it a smaller word which is a synonym e.g. destruction - ruin. All letters of the smaller word have to be in the
correct order, but not necessarily adjacent. Find the Kangaroo Words contained in the words below:

facade   hostelry   illuminated

Test Thirteen: Question 50

Solve the anagrams below. Every answer contains the letters S O L V E.

For example SOLVE + IT = VIOLETS

SOLVE + BE =   SOLVE + TIN =   SOLVE + TICK

What does the following represent?

THE
&
EEEEEEEEEEEEEEE

Which bracketed word is most opposite in meaning to the key word?

MOTTLED   (piebald, speckled, gloomy, plain, dappled)

UNLY   SED   PAA

Insert three 4-letter words into the middle of the letter arrangements to produce three words. The three 4-letter words inserted must form a familiar phrase.

Find the abbreviation, for example 9 L of a C = 9 lives of a cat

1 G T D A

The answer to the clue is a palindrome, e.g. uppermost container = top pot.

stupify crazy people

The answer to the following clues is a pair of rhyming words, for example, unhappy young man = sad lad

attractive little song

| CARIBOU | is to | mammal as a |
| GOURAMI | is to | (insect, fish, dog, plant, tree) |

Put ROD into PISTON by following these instructions and producing good English words at each stage.

		ROD
i.	change a letter	***
ii.	change a letter	***
iii	change a letter	***
iv	add three letters	PISTON

What is the longest word in the English language that can be produced from the ten letters below? No letter may be used more than once.

AMTPKLFOJC

From the following six words select the two which are opposite in meaning.

calamity, broad minded, hesitation, mustiness, ascend, bigoted

In each of the following replace two of the words or phrases in the sentence with two heteronyms without changing the meaning of the sentence, for example: The burden was our responsibility. Answer: The onus was on us.

The lady's piece of jewelry had been swallowed by the fish

Solve the following enclosure: For example: stardom in a country (4 in 6,6,2,7)
    Answer: United States o(**f Ame**)rica

fruit in a pen name (4 in 3,2,5)

Which bracketed word is most opposite in meaning to the key word?

INTERDICT   (debar, proscribe, engage, force, allow)

Add five consecutive letters of the alphabet, not necessarily in the correct order to complete the word below.

*RE***T*R

Take two of the three-letter elements and combine them to make a six-letter word which fits the keyword definition.

FOOD   (BUR, GAR, SAL, LIK, GER, AME)

Due to an over-abundance of work and current projects I exceeded an acceptable number of implements used to brand live stock in the combustible location currently in a state of ignition.

What is my current situation?

A Kangaroo word is a word which carries within it a smaller word which is a synonym e.g. destruction - ruin. All letters of the smaller word have to be in the
correct order, but not necessarily adjacent. Find the Kangaroo Words contained in the words below:

joviality   market   matches

The answer to the clue is a palindrome, e.g. uppermost container = top pot.

not in any way level

What is the longest word that can be produced from each of the two words below. Letters can only be used once each only in each word.

For example, the longest word that can be produced using the letters of the word INTERJECT no more than once each only is RETICENT.

ECONOMIST   FREQUENCY

If meat in a river (3 in 6) is T(HAM)ES can you find a particle in the human body (4 in 7)?

Find the abbreviation, for example 9 L of a C = 9 lives of a cat

2 H are B T O

What does the following represent?

Frae
Gnare
yjo

What does the following represent?

9 - all - 5

The following is an anagram of a palindromic phrase:

not snobs too (3, 2, 6)

Place the same word in front of each of these words to make five new words.

    (- - - -)   CAR
                            WAY
                            STREET
                            STEP

In the following change one letter in each word, and rearrange the order of the words to produce a familiar phrase. For example: works plan in = play on words

mob she born in

Fill in each set of brackets with two letters that finish the first word and start the second. When the correct letters have been inserted they will spell out a 10-letter word when read downwards in pairs.

MO (**) IN
TI (**) ST
TO (**) ZE
TU (**) LE
MO (**) ED

Arrange the letters of each word below to find three words which all begin with the letters QU

ITALY   TREAT   CAKED

The answer to the following clues is a pair of rhyming words, for example, unhappy young man = sad lad

extended fork point

CASINO   is to   roulette as
CATHEDRAL   is to   (worship, God, sing, assembly, preacher)

From the following six words select the two which are closest in meaning.

discharge, inclined, infrequent, flatter, occasional, persistent

If 9L of a C is nine lives of a cat, can you decode the following?

32 C on the L E

What is a DUM'DUM?

(a)	Drum	(c)	Sword
(b)	Bullet	(d)	Loose blouse

The answer to the clue is a palindrome, e.g. uppermost container = top pot.

prevent pimples

The following is an anagram of a palindromic phrase: mean moan none (4, 2, 3, 3)

In each case, change one letter only from each word to produce a familiar phrase. For example; *plan in works* would become *play on words*.

lead I hard   line is son

Solve the clue below to find a pair of words.

    W O * * *   * * * R D

Females climb gangplank

In the following change one letter in each word, and rearrange the order of the words to produce a familiar phrase. For example: works plan in = play on words

of alike dear

A Kangaroo word is a word which carries within it a smaller word which is a synonym e.g. destruction - ruin. All letters of the smaller word have to be in the
correct order, but not necessarily adjacent. Find the Kangaroo Words contained in the words below:

observe   pantaloons   perambulate

Remove a letter from a word meaning *an aviator* to leave a word meaning *a conspiracy*.

Find the abbreviation, for example 9 L of a C = 9 lives of a cat

12 P of R in the H B

Match the three letter words below with their correct meanings.

yaw, olm, nim, sou, pyx, waw, oka, lam, rya, adz, dag

a type of chest
to beat soundly or thrash
a carpenter's tool
an erratic diversion from an intended course
South American wood
a game in which matchsticks are arranged in rows

the sixth letter of the Hebrew alphabet
a European cave-dwelling salamander
a shag rug traditionally made in Sweden
the unbranched antler of a young deer
an old French copper coin

Solve the following enclosure: For example: stardom in a country (4 in 6,6,2,7)
Answer: United States o(**f Ame**)rica

capital city in a crescendo (4 in 6)

What is the longest word that can be produced from each of the two words below. Letters can only be used once each only in each word. For example, the longest word that can be produced using the letters of the word INTERJECT no more than once each only is RETICENT.

GARDENING   HUMILIATE

The answer to the following clues is a pair of rhyming words, for example, unhappy young man = sad lad

pleasingly old-fashioned holy

Find two of the three words: that can be paired to form an anagram that is a synonym of the remaining word. For example, with LEG - MEEK - NET, the words LEG and NET form an anagram of GENTLE, which is a synonym of the remaining word, MEEK.

       impound – amen – chaos

Combine three of the 3-letter bits below to produce a word meaning RADIANT

ent, per, ale, tip, ulg, ghy, eff, lye, aly, and

In the following change one letter in each word, and rearrange the order of the words to produce a familiar phrase. For example: works plan in = play on words

tumble sat pit

Complete the hyphenated word below

* * L L – L * * * * *

Place a word in the brackets that means the same as the definitions outside the brackets.

Hurl   (   )   bitumen

Find the keyword from the clues below. Numbers correspond to letters in the keyword, for example in the word another, one to seven, the word other would be represented by the numbers three to seven, and the word not would be represented by the numbers two to four.

My one to six is anger and passion,   My six to nine a standard one may ration,
My five to seven in history a span,   My whole a moderate self-restrained man.

WHEREAL   PRSITY   FTEAD

Insert three 4-letter words into the middle of the letter arrangements to produce three words. The three 4-letter words inserted must form a familiar phrase.

Add five consecutive letters of the alphabet, not necessarily in the correct order to complete the word below.

C * A * * D * W *

In each of the following replace two of the words or phrases in the sentence with two heteronyms without changing the meaning of the sentence, for example: The burden was our responsibility. Answer: The onus was on us.

The most serious people moved the large marble slabs

What does the following represent?

ov fenue

Find the abbreviation, for example 9 L of a C = 9 lives of a cat

18 H on a G C

In the following change one letter in each word, and rearrange the order of the words to produce a familiar phrase. For example: works plan in = play on words

is she soon mad

Study the following list of three words. Your task is to find the two of the three words that can be paired to form an anagram one word which is a synonym of the word remaining. For example, in the group LEG - MEEK - NET, the words LEG and NET are an anagram of GENTLE, which is a synonym of the remaining word MEEK.

care - tale - cut

From the following six words select the two which are opposite in meaning.

onerous, motion, adipose, light, unseal, force

Add a letter to the beginning and end of a tree to produce an early type of harpsichord.

What is the longest word that can be produced from each of the two words below. Letters can only be used once each only in each word. For example, the longest word that can be produced using the letters of the word INTERJECT no more than once each only is RETICENT.

IMPUDENCE
JUXTAPOSE

The answer to the following clues is a pair of rhyming words, for example, unhappy young man = sad lad

sylvan flower seller

The answer to the clue is a palindrome, e.g. uppermost container = top pot.

stately beer

Take two of the three-letter elements and combine them to make a six-letter word which fits the keyword definition.

DANCE   (CHE, MIN, CHA, CAM, UET, CAW)

Find the abbreviation, for example 9 L of a C = 9 lives of a cat

3 M in a B by J K J

Add one letter of the alphabet to the word NURSE, and then rearrange the six resultant letters to find the name of a famous painter.

Solve the following enclosure: For example: stardom in a country (4 in 6,6,2,7)
       Answer: United States o(**f Ame**)rica

country in a container for hatching eggs (4 in 9)

A Kangaroo word is a word which carries within it a smaller word which is a synonym e.g. destruction - ruin. All letters of the smaller word have to be in the
correct order, but not necessarily adjacent. Find the Kangaroo Words contained in the words below:

perimeter   prattle   precipitation

Find a reason to arrange these words in six pairs.

Arian, mature, tier, lever, Libra, table, front, hives, rage, port, arm, arch

In each case, change one letter only from each word to produce a familiar phrase. For example; *plan in works* would become *play on words*.

met an army
noon fight

The following is an anagram of a palindromic phrase:

redden over oven (5, 3, 2, 4)

Find the abbreviation, for example 9 L of a C = 9 lives of a cat

11 L a L in the T D C

What is the longest word that can be produced from each of the two words below. Letters can only be used once each only in each word.

For example, the longest word that can be produced using the letters of the word INTERJECT no more than once each only is RETICENT.

KISSOGRAM
LAUGHABLE

Solve the anagrams (all 12-letter words) and say what they all have in common.

peanut bricks	boards nicely	should remain
Bordeaux mist	unsocial debt	

From the following six words select the two which are closest in meaning.

rapacious, innuendo, imprint, brutal, inscribe, indiscreet

Use every letter of the phrase HAPPILY RARE SUPERB once each only to produce three precious stones.

Add one letter of the alphabet to the word SIESTA, and then rearrange the seven resultant letters to find the name of a famous painter.

Homonyms are words which are spelled differently but are pronounced the same for example: son and sun. Find a pair of homonyms for the clues.

channel / direct

Change the first word into the second word by finding a link at each stage, for example, the word HAND can be changed to GLOVE by proceeding: HAND – OUT – FOX – GLOVE.

Go from CROSS to WORD

CROSS
* * U N * R *
* U * I *
* O *
C * *
J * * *
* N I * *
P * * N *
* * *
* O O *
* E *
W O R D

What is an ENCYCLICAL?

    (a)   Enclosure
    (b)   Pope's letter
    (c)   Illness
    (d)   Arab prince

The answer to the following clues is a pair of rhyming words, for example, unhappy young man = sad lad

nocturnally clear

AFGI

Add four consecutive letters of the alphabet and then rearrange the eight resultant letters to produce an exotic bird (8 letters)

Complete the names of the eight animals (only alternate letters have been shown). Then rearrange the first letters of each of the animals to find a ninth animal.

```
* E * N * E * R
* Y * L *
* P * S * U *
* O * I * L *
* O * L *
* N * G * R
* N * E * O * E
* R * A * I * L *
```

Place the same word in front of each of these words to make five new words.

(- - - - -) POSE
MINGLE
PLAY
MISSION
ACT

Add a letter to the beginning and end of an incline to make things moderately cold.

Solve the following enclosure:

For example: stardom in a country (4 in 6,6,2,7)
Answer: United States o(**f Ame**)rica

European capital city in an analogy (5 in 10)

The answer to the clue is a palindrome, e.g. uppermost container = top pot.

the menace transgressed

Find the abbreviation, for example 9 L of a C = 9 lives of a cat

4 U S P on M R

Test Fifteen: Question 39

Add one letter of the alphabet to the word UPDATES, and then rearrange the eight resultant letters to find a capital city.

Test Fifteen: Question 40

What does the following represent?

out
and

Test Fifteen: Question 41

Homonyms are words which are spelled differently but are pronounced the same for example: son and sun. Find a pair of homonyms for the clues.

revolve / seabird

Test Fifteen: Question 42

The object outside the brackets always has two of the features inside the brackets. Identify which two

Omnibus (people, wheels, number plate, driver, conductor)

Test Fifteen: Question 43

Use all 21 letters once each only to spell out the names of three types of bird.

REINFORCING SHAKY BRAIN

DILLTU

Add four consecutive letters of the alphabet and then rearrange the ten resultant letters to produce a ten-letter word meaning charming.

Insert two consecutive letters of the alphabet into the beginning, middle or end of the following to create a word

boat

In the following change one letter in each word, and rearrange the order of the words to produce a familiar phrase. For example: works plan in = play on words

she done wider

Of the following five words, four have a common theme. Which is the odd one out?

orange, pear, peach, grape, damson

Find the abbreviation, for example 9 L of a C = 9 lives of a cat

6 P on a P T

Study the following list of three words. Your task is to find the two of the three words that can be paired to form an anagram one word which is a synonym of the word remaining. For example, in the group LEG - MEEK - NET, the words LEG and NET are an anagram of GENTLE, which is a synonym of the remaining word MEEK.

point - creep - idea

Nine radishes is an anagram of which well-known phrase (4, 3, 5)

Which two words that are pronounced the same but are spelled differently mean *conveyed* and *redolence*?

What is the longest word that can be produced from each of the two words below. Letters can only be used once each only in each word. For example, the longest word that can be produced using the letters of the word INTERJECT no more than once each only is RETICENT.

MARSUPIAL
NOVELTIES

Which bracketed word is most opposite in meaning to the key word?

WRATHFUL   (subdue, futile, incensed, furious, serene)

A Kangaroo word is a word which carries within it a smaller word which is a synonym e.g. destruction - ruin. All letters of the smaller word have to be in the correct order, but not necessarily adjacent. Find the Kangaroo Words contained in the words below:

rapscallion   recline   regulates

The answer to the following clues is a pair of rhyming words, for example, unhappy young man = sad lad

ensconse money

Homonyms are words which are spelled differently but are pronounced the same for example: son and sun. Find a pair of homonyms for the clues.

coast / tree

In each case, change one letter only from each word to produce a familiar phrase. For example; *plan in works* would become *play on words*.

then of toy
cove so I hear

Insert two consecutive letters of the alphabet   into the beginning, middle or end of the following to create a word

aost

Find the abbreviation, for example 9 L of a C = 9 lives of a cat

7 B for S B

From the following six words select the two which are opposite in meaning.

methodical, primitive, arrogant, disorderly, apparent, admit

Solve the following enclosure:

For example: stardom in a country (4 in 6,6,2,7)
                      Answer: United States o(**f Ame**)rica

mountain range in emission of light (5 in 13)

A Kangaroo word is a word which carries within it a smaller word which is a synonym e.g. destruction - ruin. All letters of the smaller word have to be in the
correct order, but not necessarily adjacent. Find the Kangaroo Words contained in the words below:

revolution
rotund
salvage

The answer to the clue is a palindrome, e.g. uppermost container = top pot.

doddering cats

In the following change one letter in each word, and rearrange the order of the words to produce a familiar phrase. For example: works plan in = play on words

I ore mast full

Study the following list of three words. Your task is to find the two of the three words that can be paired to form an anagram one word which is a synonym of the word remaining. For example, in the group LEG - MEEK - NET, the words LEG and NET are an anagram of GENTLE, which is a synonym of the remaining word MEEK.

state - fair - denote

Take two of the three-letter elements and combine them to make a six-letter word which fits the keyword definition.

                   SPORT   (ROW, SOC, INK, SQU, CER, ASK)

In the following change one letter in each word, and rearrange the order of the words to produce a familiar phrase. For example: works plan in = play on words

ten if she slit

Insert two consecutive letters of the alphabet into the beginning, middle or end of the following to create a word

                              mae

Each of the following word combinations rhymes with a well-known phrase, for example fight and play rhymes with night and day. Can you work out the two phrases?

disbar and fried   sever and gone

From the following six words select the two which are closest in meaning.

conceal, hooked, devoutness, discharge, aquiline, extensive

EIOPPR

Add four consecutive letters of the alphabet and then rearrange the ten resultant letters to produce a ten-letter word meaning giving assistance.

Find the abbreviation, for example 9 L of a C = 9 lives of a cat

14 L in a S

Homonyms are words which are spelled differently but are pronounced the same
for example: son and sun. Find a pair of homonyms for the clues.

inlet / harsh squeak

Study the following list of three words. Your task is to find the two of the three words that can be paired to form an anagram one word which is a synonym of the word remaining. For example, in the group LEG - MEEK - NET, the words LEG and NET are an anagram of GENTLE, which is a synonym of the remaining word MEEK.

undo - glad - intense

In the following change one letter in each word, and rearrange the order of the words to produce a familiar phrase. For example: works plan in = play on words

is ill ale

Of the following five words, four have a common theme. Which is the odd one out?

tarpon, corvette, galliass, trimaran, schooner

Place a word in the brackets that means the same as the definitions outside the brackets.

Origin   (   )   rummage

Find two of the three words: that can be paired to form an anagram that is a synonym of the remaining word. For example, with LEG - MEEK - NET, the words LEG and NET form an anagram of GENTLE, which is a synonym of the remaining word, MEEK.

     ram – liken - cope

What is an EMETIC?

     (a)   Figured glass
     (b)   Plant
     (c)   Medicine
     (d)   Mound or ridge

cart, split, line, age

Which word below has something in common with all the words above?

minimum, profit, stone, cast

What is the longest word that can be produced from each of the two words below. Letters can only be used once each only in each word.

For example, the longest word that can be produced using the letters of the word INTERJECT no more than once each only is RETICENT.

OMBUDSMAN
PIROUETTE

Place the same word in front of each of these words to make five new words.

```
( - - - )          GOING
                   WARD
                   STAY
                   SIDE
                   POUR
```

Solve the following enclosure: For example: stardom in a country (4 in 6,6,2,7)
          Answer: United States o(**f Ame**)rica

insect in a tycoon (4 in 7)

Study the following list of three words. Your task is to find the two of the three words that can be paired to form an anagram one word which is a synonym of the word remaining. For example, in the group LEG - MEEK - NET, the words LEG and NET are an anagram of GENTLE, which is a synonym of the remaining word MEEK.

hint - verve - assume

Homonyms are words which are spelled differently but are pronounced the same for example: son and sun. Find a pair of homonyms for the clues.

cringe / rural deity

Insert three consecutive letters of the alphabet into the beginning, middle or end of the following to create a word

ine

The answer to the clue is a palindrome, e.g. uppermost container = top pot.

spacious wasteland

Add one letter of the alphabet to the word CANONISE, and then rearrange the nine resultant letters to find the name of an island in the Atlantic Ocean.

In each case, change one letter only from each word to produce a familiar phrase. For example; *plan in works* would become *play on words*.

newer sad due
wide end done

Find the abbreviation, for example 9 L of a C = 9 lives of a cat

19 to the D

The object outside the brackets always has two of the features inside the brackets. Identify which two

River (fish, ducks, water, river bank, boats)

In the following change one letter in each word, and rearrange the order of the words to produce a familiar phrase. For example: works plan in = play on words

is live at barge

Insert three consecutive letters of the alphabet into the beginning, middle or end of the following to create a word

aan

Each of the following word combinations rhymes with a well-known phrase, for example fight and play rhymes with night and day. Can you work out the two phrases?

cheer and row   gnome and why

Solve the following line by line to reveal an eight-letter word.

My first is in duplicate and also copies,
My second's in flowers as well as poppies,
My third is in rectify and correction,
My fourth is in patience and perfection,
My fifth is in project but not in plan,
My sixth is in woman and also man,
My seventh's in description but not in fact,
My eighth's in position and also intact,
Now its complete, so what can it be,
A reminder perhaps of what we see.

Study the following list of three words. Your task is to find the two of the three words that can be paired to form an anagram one word which is a synonym of the word remaining. For example, in the group LEG - MEEK - NET, the words LEG and NET are an anagram of GENTLE, which is a synonym of the remaining word MEEK.

elicit - oval - pall

page   ?   hem   line   age

What word is missing?

Find the abbreviation, for example 9 L of a C = 9 lives of a cat

8 K of E C H

A familiar saying has been split into three-letter groups. What is the saying?

ORE   OFB   SAJ   ATH   OYF   ING   EAU   VER   TYI

Solve the clue below to find a pair of words.

     P L * *   * * * A Y

Scheme at the present time

Add one letter of the alphabet to the word BOATMAN, and then rearrange the eight resultant letters to find the name of a Canadian province.

AAEIOPT

Add four consecutive letters of the alphabet and then rearrange the eleven resultant letters to produce an eleven-letter word meaning propensity to steal.

Homonyms are words which are spelled differently but are pronounced the same for example: son and sun. Find a pair of homonyms for the clues.

occasion / moments

Which four bits can be joined together to produce two words that have opposite meanings?

ast, eer, pur, lon, ify, wil, oul, all, ore, bef

What is the longest word that can be produced from each of the two words below. Letters can only be used once each only in each word.

For example, the longest word that can be produced using the letters of the word INTERJECT no more than once each only is RETICENT.

QUALIFIED
REPREHEND

Insert three consecutive letters of the alphabet into the beginning, middle or end of the following to create a word

sing

ACEEMOTU

Add the same letter four times to the above group of letters and then rearrange the twelve resultant letters to produce a twelve-letter word meaning proclamation.

From the following six words select the two which are opposite in meaning.

restrain, priority, preface, mandate, exaltation, appendix

In the following change one letter in each word, and rearrange the order of the words to produce a familiar phrase. For example: works plan in = play on words

fill heals doll

Study the following list of three words. Your task is to find the two of the three words that can be paired to form an anagram one word which is a synonym of the word remaining. For example, in the group LEG - MEEK - NET, the words LEG and NET are an anagram of GENTLE, which is a synonym of the remaining word MEEK.

toys - hoarse - seer

Each of the following word combinations rhymes with a well-known phrase, for example fight and play rhymes with night and day. Can you work out the two phrases?

Asquith and Edwin
grip and struck

Insert three consecutive letters of the alphabet into the beginning, middle or end of the following to create a word

ack

Use each letter of the sentence:

O my ! Botanical ape. Boo!!

once each only to spell out three kinds of animal.

The answer to the clue is a palindrome, e.g. uppermost container = top pot.

burst forth unadulterated

Add one letter of the alphabet to the word ROMPERS, and then rearrange the eight resultant letters to find the name of a type of flower.

Test Seventeen: Question 16

Take two of the three-letter elements and combine them to make a six-letter word which fits the keyword definition.

OCCUPATIONS   (JOI, JOC, GRO, SER, NIR, KEY)

Test Seventeen: Question 17

Select two words that are synonyms, plus an antonym of these two synonyms, from the list of words below.

inflexible, irrational, unsound, judicious, irretrievable, abnormal

Test Seventeen: Question 18

From the following six words select the two which are closest in meaning.

gratuity, estimable, solemnise, granting, unavailing, endowment

Test Seventeen: Question 19

Find the abbreviation, for example 9 L of a C = 9 lives of a cat

15 M of F per P

Test Seventeen: Question 20

```
   *      *      *      *      *      *      *
   L      O      W      V      O      C      R
   S      O      I      A      V      O      I
   *      *      *      *      *      *      *
```

Insert two countries, one on the top line and one on the bottom line to produce seven four-letter words reading downwards

In the following change one letter in each word, and rearrange the order of the words to produce a familiar phrase. For example: works plan in = play on words

four got in line

Insert three consecutive letters of the alphabet into the beginning, middle or end of the following to create a word

caess

Homonyms are words which are spelled differently but are pronounced the same, e.g. son and sun. Find a pair of homonyms for the clues.

gait / Asiatic grassland

In each case, change one letter only from each word to produce a familiar phrase. For example; *plan in works* would become *play on words*.

aim on are   put at put

Place the same word in front of each of these words to make five new words.

(- -)   TER
                       FORMAL
                       LET
                       FORM

Insert three consecutive letters of the alphabet into the beginning, middle or end of the following to create a word

solent

What is the longest word that can be produced from each of the two words below. Letters can only be used once each only in each word. For example, the longest word that can be produced using the letters of the word INTERJECT no more than once each only is RETICENT.

SIGNIFIED   TURBULENT

Combine three of the 3-letter bits below to produce a word meaning a period of three months.

end, car, mes, imp, rye, ter, ale, art, tri, enn

A Kangaroo word is a word which carries within it a smaller word which is a synonym e.g. destruction - ruin. All letters of the smaller word have to be in the
correct order, but not necessarily adjacent. Find the Kangaroo Words contained in the words below:

satisfied   splotches
separate   supervisor

What is a FINNAN?

     (a)   Young duckling   (c)   Haddock
     (b)   Musical instrument   (d)   Large mammal

Many words have dropped out of common usage, but still appear as idioms as part of other words, or with prefixes and suffixes attached. An example of such a word is ruthless, in which the meaning of the little-used word *ruth* is compassion. In the following words and expressions can you spot the fossilized word, and work out its correct meaning as a stand-alone word?

short shrift   rank and file   out of kilter

Which is the odd one out?

mustard oil, alkyd resin, choux pastry, magnetic flux, venus flytrap, talcum powder, brazil nut, sodium chlorate, musk orchid, prickly ash.

FOX   is to   fur as
CROCODILE   is to   (scales, skin, tail, teeth, jaws)

first of all
starting block
a fifth of scotch
the end of the world
the beginning of the end
starting friction
the middle of the night

What comes next?

next of kin, the middle of nowhere, two of a kind, second in command, the start of something big.

Add two letters of the alphabet to the word CHLORITE, and then rearrange the ten resultant letters to find the name of a form of transportation.

AIP

Add the same letter four times to the above group of letters and then rearrange the seven resultant letters to produce a seven-letter word meaning oomph.

Which bracketed word is most opposite in meaning to the key word?

CHAFE   (sooth, gall, irritate, confine, ruffle)

Change a pair of double letters in a word meaning a mother superior to another pair of double letters to produce a word meaning the right to enter.

Place a word in the brackets that means the same as the definitions outside the brackets.

Secure   (   )   go hungry

In doing what most would describe as easy I am in a state of enlightenment and prudence despite the set of circumstances that occupy my current thoughts having already elapsed. What am I doing?

crate, repel, elope, least, ether

What comes next?

paint, truce, thread, paper, brush

Find the abbreviation, for example 9 L of a C = 9 lives of a cat

10 F in T P B

The object outside the brackets always has two of the features inside the brackets. Identify which two

Bird (whistle, plumage, eyes, legs, beak)

hill   rock
roof   tree
black   false
table   river

Which two words are in the wrong columns?

Change one letter only in each word below to form a familiar phrase.

SEA EVE SO ERE

YOUR DECREPIT ROMP is an anagram of which two words that are similar in meaning?

Which of the following is not an anagram of a type of deer?

ONE LEAPT
FILL WIDE
TREK COB
DIRE ERNE

Complete the hyphenated word below.

* * * E – E F F * * *

Clue: secondary

What commonality is shared by the words STREWN and PROPERTY?

The answer to the clue is a palindrome, e.g. uppermost container = top pot.

less than adequate slouch

Homonyms are words which are spelled differently but are pronounced the same for example: son and sun. Find a pair of homonyms for the clues.

ritual / correct

Insert three consecutive letters of the alphabet into the beginning, middle or end of the following to create a word

cay

conveyer, marmalade, eclipse, telegram, photoelectric

Which two words are in the wrong order in the above list?

If meat in a river (3 in 6) is T(HAM)ES can you find a direction in the sternum (4 in 10)?

What three letters come next?

BM ALELT TILA DAHY ***

The clue *revoke alliance* leads to which pair of rhyming words?

From the following six words select the two which are opposite in meaning.

ravenous, satisfied, sensitive, efface, excellent, enrapture

Study the following list of three words. Your task is to find the two of the three words that can be paired to form an anagram one word which is a synonym of the word remaining. For example, in the group LEG - MEEK - NET, the words LEG and NET are an anagram of GENTLE, which is a synonym of the remaining word MEEK.

jig - arc - pen

Insert three consecutive letters of the alphabet into the beginning, middle or end of the following to create a word

thiy

In the following change one letter in each word, and rearrange the order of the words to produce a familiar phrase. For example: works plan in = play on words

so plan set hand

The answer to the clue is a palindrome, e.g. uppermost container = top pot.

social gathering allurement

DOCTOR	is to	hospital as
SCHOOL MASTER	is to	(teaching, study, school, lessons, learning)

In each case, change one letter only from each word to produce a familiar phrase. For example; *plan in works* would become *play on words*.

rome any bet is   fan any side

Change one letter in each word, and rearrange the order of the words to produce a familiar phrase, e.g. works plan in = play on words

but stem on link

Take two of the three-letter elements and combine them to make a six-letter word which fits the keyword definition.

MILITARY   (BAT, CON, ESC, TLE, BIT, AUT)

Change one letter only in each word below to form a familiar phrase.
LAD GOWN SHE SAW

Which two words that sound alike but share no letters mean a female of the genus ovis and the pronoun of the second person?

Test Eighteen: Question 18

What is the longest word that can be produced from each of the two words below. Letters can only be used once each only in each word. For example, the longest word that can be produced using the letters of the word INTERJECT no more than once each only is RETICENT.

UNIVERSAL   VENTILATE

Test Eighteen: Question 19

PACE   TRUE

Add one letter to each word above to produce two words similar in meaning.

Test Eighteen: Question 20

Insert three consecutive letters of the alphabet into the beginning, middle or end of the following to create a word

ate

Test Eighteen: Question 21

From the following six words select the two which are closest in meaning.

obviate, headstrong, independent, possessive, eradicate, avert

Test Eighteen: Question 22

Find the abbreviation, for example 9 L of a C = 9 lives of a cat: 16 P on a C B

Test Eighteen: Question 23

Place a word in the brackets that means the same as the definitions outside the brackets.

Satisfactory   (   )   penalty

If 9L of a C is nine lives of a cat, can you decode the following?

2 M in a W N

Insert a word in the brackets so that it completes a word or phrase when tacked onto the word on the left and completes another word or phrase when placed in front of the word on the right.

Slap   (   )   medium

The answer to the clue is a palindrome, e.g. uppermost container = top pot.

more than six evenings

What is a GRANAM?

(a)   Type of gravy   (c)   Type of cloth
(b)   Musical instrument   (d)   Water-fly

Place the same word in front of each of these words to make five new words.

(- - -)   SALT
                 WEED
                 MEN
                 SIDE
                 SON

Only one group of five letters below can be arranged to spell out a five-letter word in the English language. Find the word.

WOCLE   ABTWI   UWLON
HUANP   FLITO   ABRIN

Complete the hyphenated word below

* * * * O – O P P * * * * * * * *

Clue: publicity

Complete the words with the aid of the clues. The letters XYZ in each word are the same three letters which spell out a three-letter word.

X Y Z * * *   wavelet
* X Y Z * *   type of frame or stand
* * X Y Z *   written document
* * * X Y Z   fit a new holding device as on a golf club

What phrase (6, 2, 10) is indicated by the arrangement of letters below?

* * * R A C T * * *

Insert a word in the brackets so that it completes a word or phrase when tacked onto the word on the left and completes another word or phrase when placed in front of the word on the right.

Sea   (   )   net

What is the longest word that can be produced from each of the two words below. Letters can only be used once each only in each word. For example, the longest word that can be produced using the letters of the word INTERJECT no more than once each only is RETICENT.

WINDSWEPT
XYLORIMBA

Insert four consecutive letters of the alphabet into the beginning, middle or end of the following to create a word

undedy

The answer to the clue is a palindrome, e.g. uppermost container = top pot.

hauled forward

Homonyms are words which are spelled differently but are pronounced the same for example: son and sun. Find a pair of homonyms for the clues.

manner / revealing

Test Eighteen: Question 38

Which bracketed word is most similar in meaning to the key word?

HERALD (devil, guide, guard, messenger, flock)

Test Eighteen: Question 39

Fill in the blanks to create three words which are anagrams

*L*E* A***T **T*R

Test Eighteen: Question 40

In the following change one letter in each word, and rearrange the order of the words to produce a familiar phrase. For example: works plan in = play on words

now by so on do me

Test Eighteen: Question 41

The object outside the brackets always has two of the features inside the brackets. Identify which two

Island (water, trees, land, natives, birds)

Test Eighteen: Question 42

Many words have dropped out of common usage, but still appear as idioms as part of other words, or with prefixes and suffixes attached. An example of such a word is ruthless, in which the meaning of the little-used word *ruth* is compassion. In the following words and expressions can you spot the fossilized word, and work out its correct meaning as a stand-alone word?

kit and kaboodle
footpad
raring to go

Test Eighteen: Question 43

I have availed myself of the opportunity to seize with the bony appendages of the jaws a fleshy drupe from the tree of the genus Prunus for the occasion which exceeds the first in value. What have I done?

Test Eighteen: Question 44

If meat in a river (3 in 6) is T(HAM)ES can you find a Roman god in paraffin (4 in 8)?

Test Eighteen: Question 45

In the following change one letter in each word, and rearrange the order of the words to produce a familiar phrase. For example: works plan in = play on words

cars hate malls

Test Eighteen: Question 46

Insert a word in the brackets so that it completes a word or phrase when tacked onto the word on the left and completes another word or phrase when placed in front of the word on the right.

can   (   )   not

Test Eighteen: Question 47

Complete the five words below which are all similar in meaning.

```
* U * * I * A * E *
* U A * E
* O * * I * * I * A * E *
U * * A * E
* E F * N * D
```

DEY   REE   COME   REED

What three-letter word can be inserted into the letter arrangements above to produce four words?

Fill in the blanks to create three words which are anagrams

*E*V*   *E**R   ****S

Homonyms are words which are spelled differently but are pronounced the same for example: son and sun. Find a pair of homonyms for the clues.

pretend / willing

Change one letter only in each word below to form a familiar phrase.

SIT US SHOW

Add four consecutive letters of the alphabet, not necessarily in the correct order to complete the word below.

P * O * E C * * E

The name of which animal (6 letters), usually associated with the winter, can be produced from the letters:

W   I   N   T   E   R   T   I   M   E

Place a word in the brackets that means the same as the definitions outside the brackets.

Non-professional   (   )   a ballad

Use every letter of the phrase A SMILING BEAST once each only to spell out three types of herb.

DOY, BAL, SNY, SLY, HAY, GRY, ?

What three letters come next?

Find a sequence that can be added to these words, when combined into five pairs, to produce five new words:

fold, rant, mount, head, perm, par, corm, man, for, table

ocelot, nozzle, dental, jackal

What comes next?

fasten, cheese, Africa, feudal, monkey

If meat in a river (3 in 6) is T(HAM)ES can you find a thoroughfare in a radio message (4 in 9)?

Which bracketed word is most opposite in meaning to the key word?

WASPISH   (snappish, moist, cautious, patient, violent)

If 9L of a C is nine lives of a cat, can you decode the following?

300 for a P S in T- P B

From the following six words select the two which are opposite in meaning.

sever, obscurity, join, spectral, imply, imitation

Which nine-letter word contains the repeated letter sequence OTOT?

* * O T O T * * *

Take two of the three-letter elements and combine them to make a six-letter word which fits the keyword definition.

TRANSPORT   (AIR, GLI, ROC, CET, DAR, BUS)

Find two of the three words: that can be paired to form an anagram that is a synonym of the remaining word. For example, with LEG - MEEK - NET, the words LEG and NET form an anagram of GENTLE, which is a synonym of the remaining word, MEEK.

Art – etch – cog

A I L M

Add four consecutive letters of the alphabet and then rearrange the eight resultant letters to produce an eight-letter word meaning unselfishness.

Which four bits can be joined together to produce two words that have opposite meanings?

ure, ail, too, ime, fut, lie, for, ere, mer, ine

As a result of my cheery disposition I am making a kind of musical sound by forcing my breath through a small orifice formed by contracting the lips at the same time that I am exerting intellectual or physical effort directed to an end result. What am I doing?

Place a word in the brackets that means the same as the definitions outside the brackets.

Fair   (   )   very recently

From the following six words select the two which are closest in meaning.

saunter, surfeit, scared, preserve, lucid, ramble

Place the same word in front of each of these words to make five new words.

      (- -)   TACK
                                   TIRE
                                   TEMPT
                                   TEST
                                   TUNE

BLNSTVY

Add the same letter five times to the above group of letters and then rearrange the twelve resultant letters to produce a twelve-letter word meaning a state of not being perceivable.

Combine three of the three letter bits to produce a word meaning a tune which repeats a simple strain.

        eat   ate   our   rou   ety   nde   air   lay   pin

      SCH   BEE   SIC

Insert three 3-letter words into the middle of the letter arrangements to produce three 6-letter words. The three 3-letter words inserted must form a familiar phrase.

Change a pair of double letters in a word meaning combatant to another pair of double letters to produce a word meaning chatterbox.

Place a word in the brackets that means the same as the definitions outside the brackets.

Establisher   (   )   break down or fail

Solve the anagrams below which all contain the letters C A S E, for example CASE + BEN = absence

CASE + RIB
CASE + ROT
CASE + STY
CASE + LIP

Test Nineteen: Question 28

Complete the words below which all are similar in meaning.

* * O * A *
I * * E * * A * I O * A *
U * I * E * * A *
* O * * * * I * E

Test Nineteen: Question 29

What is GINGIVAL?

(a)   Maidenhead tree
(b)   Of the gums
(c)   Knick-knack
(d)   Japanese board game

Test Nineteen: Question 30

Insert a word in the brackets so that it completes a word or phrase when tacked onto the word on the left and completes another word or phrase when placed in front of the word on the right.

No   (   )   now

Test Nineteen: Question 31

Add four consecutive letters of the alphabet, not necessarily in the correct order to complete the word below.

C H A * * I * *

EGHOORR

Add four consecutive letters of the alphabet and then rearrange the eleven resultant letters to produce an eleven-letter word meaning agitated.

Which four bits can be joined together to produce two words that have opposite meanings?

bia, ere, rip, ort, lik, shy, pho, aly, ent, ing

AEESU

Add the same letter four times to the above group of letters and then rearrange the nine resultant letters to produce a nine-letter word meaning a small figure.

Change a pair of double letters in a word meaning felon to another pair of double letters to produce a word meaning a small inlet.

AALN

Add four consecutive letters of the alphabet and then rearrange the eight resultant letters to produce an eight-letter word meaning equal.

Add four consecutive letters of the alphabet, not necessarily in the correct order to complete the word below.

* * | * | * E

Which bracketed word is most similar in meaning to the key word?

OBSTINACY   (perseverence, docility, security, urgency, inferring)

Which two words that sound alike but are spelled differently mean morally pure and hunted.

K O P R

Add four consecutive letters of the alphabet and then rearrange the eight resultant letters to produce an eight-letter word meaning scenery.

Of the following five words, four have a common theme. Which is the odd one out?

gold, tin, iron, aluminium, copper

The object outside the brackets always has two of the features inside the brackets. Identify which two

Book (author, title, pages, letters, cover)

park, boy, point

What word below has something in common with all the words above?

search, dispute, room, carrot, tack

Add four consecutive letters of the alphabet, not necessarily in the correct order to complete the word below.

*E**UI*ITE

Which four bits can be joined together to produce two words that have opposite meanings?

ary, ile, dam, pos, air, bie, ous, ine, rep, age

AEGIY

Add the same letter four times to the above group of letters and then rearrange the nine resultant letters to produce a nine-letter word meaning unlawfully.

Solve the anagrams below which all contain the letters C A S E, for example CASE + BEN = absence

CASE + ROLF =
CASE + MAIN =
CASE + TALE =
CASE + MINT =

Add a letter to the beginning and end of a delicate fabric to find locations.

The answer to the following clues is a pair of rhyming words, for example, unhappy young man = sad lad

instruct discourse

Work from letter to adjacent letter Boggle-style to find a phrase.
Letters can be used more than once, and each letter is used at least once.

```
A    U    A    D
T    R    M    L
T    I    O    S
E    Y    C    N
```

Study the following list of three words. Your task is to find the two of the three words that can be paired to form an anagram one word which is a synonym of the word remaining. For example, in the group LEG - MEEK - NET, the words LEG and NET are an anagram of GENTLE, which is a synonym of the remaining word MEEK.

buy - edge - adorn

If 9L of a C is nine lives of a cat, can you decode the following?

7 P in a W P T

RIDGE   NER   IES

Which four-letter word can precede all the above to produce three words?

EL, ON, AGE, OON, RIDGE

What four-letter word can be placed in front of the above to produce five words?

What is the longest word that can be produced from each of the two words below. Letters can only be used once each only in each word. For example, the longest word that can be produced using the letters of the word INTERJECT no more than once each only is RETICENT.

YODELLING
ZOOLOGIST

What word meaning STURDY means SHOULD when its first letter is moved to last?

DEMONIACAL ROTTER is an anagram of which two words that are similar in meaning?

aid
wind
world
estate
column
sense
?

What word comes next?

cardinal, sky, cloud, picture, heaven, mystery

Fill in the blanks to create three words which are anagrams

I*E   *M*   **L*S

From the following six words select the two which are opposite in meaning.

solemnise, desert, resolution, mitigate, association, profane

Find two of the three words: that can be paired to form an anagram that is a synonym of the remaining word. For example, with LEG - MEEK - NET, the words LEG and NET form an anagram of GENTLE, which is a synonym of the remaining word, MEEK.

Bale – fit – cap

Study the following list of three words. Your task is to find the two of the three words that can be paired to form an anagram one word which is a synonym of the word remaining. For example, in the group LEG - MEEK - NET, the words LEG and NET are an anagram of GENTLE, which is a synonym of the remaining word MEEK.

army - scout - usual

Homonyms are words which are spelled differently but are pronounced the same, e.g. son and sun. Find a pair of homonyms for the clues.

chamber / tug

In the following change one letter in each word, and rearrange the order of the words to produce a familiar phrase. For example: works plan in = play on words

cut on rear dear

Take two of the three-letter elements and combine them to make a six-letter word which fits the keyword.

GIRL'S NAMES   (GRA, PET, TRI, CEY, XIY, ULA)

Study the following list of three words. Your task is to find the two of the three words that can be paired to form an anagram one word which is a synonym of the word remaining. For example, in the group LEG - MEEK - NET, the words LEG and NET are an anagram of GENTLE, which is a synonym of the remaining word MEEK.

sooner - series - grips

Each of the following word combinations rhymes with a well-known phrase, for example fight and play rhymes with night and day. Can you work out the two phrases?

allow and pen   rover and shout

Study the following list of three words. Your task is to find the two of the three words that can be paired to form an anagram one word which is a synonym of the word remaining. For example, in the group LEG - MEEK - NET, the words LEG and NET are an anagram of GENTLE, which is a synonym of the remaining word MEEK.

era - wax - since

Fill in the blanks to create three words which are anagrams

*IL**   S**N*   ***K*

Each of the following word combinations rhymes with a well-known phrase, for example fight and play rhymes with night and day. Can you work out the two phrases?

butch and slow   grate and Capri

What phrase is represented by the arrangement of letters and dots below?

****E R   M A D****

Homonyms are words which are spelled differently but are pronounced the same
for example: son and sun. Find a pair of homonyms for the clues.

encroach / forcefully protested

From the following six words select the two which are closest in meaning.

lampoon, mishap, modify, hesitate, gloomy, satirise

Solve the anagram in brackets (7, 10) to find a famous event of the 20th century.

the (universal riot on us)

Study the following list of three words. Your task is to find the two of the three words that can be paired
to form an anagram one word which is a synonym of the word remaining. For example, in the group LEG
- MEEK - NET, the words LEG and NET are an anagram of GENTLE, which is a synonym of the remaining
word MEEK.

hope - master - air

Of the following five words, four have a common theme. Which is the odd one out?

beech, oak, fir, sycamore, teak

Place the same word in front of each of these words to make five new words.

(- - - -)   GROUND
                    MATE
                    TIME
                    LET
                    PEN

Fill in the blanks to create three words which are anagrams

*ES**   *T*E*   *R***

Add a letter to the beginning and end of radiance to make capricious.

What is GOBY?

      (a)   Fish
      (b)   Desert
      (c)   Wooden beam
      (d)   Flower

The clues *a fortified place* and *accent* lead to which pair of words that are anagrams of each other?

Apart from slang words there are only ten parts of the body that are spelled with three letters. One of these is jaw. Use each of the remaining nine once each only to complete the following words.

al *** e	ve *** s	d *** ble	s *** ch	w *** ly
cal *** er	ob *** d	ar *** ent	w *** ped	

Each three-word phrase has been hidden by removing the initial letters of each word and then removing the space between them. For example *odds and ends* would become DDSNDNDS.

HANGEFEART   ORGETEOT   ALLFIRRORS

Study the following list of three words. Your task is to find the two of the three words that can be paired to form an anagram one word which is a synonym of the word remaining. For example, in the group LEG - MEEK - NET, the words LEG and NET are an anagram of GENTLE, which is a synonym of the remaining word MEEK.

woe - teach - hear

Homonyms are words which are spelled differently but are pronounced the same for example: son and sun. Find a pair of homonyms for the clues.

lift / thin beams of light

Each three-word phrase has been hidden by removing the initial letters of each word and then removing the space between them. For example *odds and ends* would become DDSNDNDS

BSENTITHOUTEAVE
LLNLL
HREEAYVENT

What word can be added to the beginning
end or middle of the words below to create new words or phrases?

mail   sing   bearer   rest

Find a reason for arranging these ten words into five groups of two words each.

vision, access, column, Indian, plated, random, spinal, summer, tunnel, armour

Each three-word phrase has been hidden by removing the initial letters of each word and then removing the space between them. For example *odds and ends* would become DDSNDNDS

ALLSAVEARS   URNHEABLES   IMEFTERIME

The object outside the brackets always has two of the features inside the brackets. Identify which two

Clock (numbers, hands, works, chime, feet)

Fill in the blanks to create three words which are anagrams

P****   **A*E   L***T

ISLAND   is to sea as
PENINSULAR is to (land, shore, sand, rocks, jutting)

Homonyms are words which are spelled differently but are pronounced the same
for example: son and sun. Find a pair of homonyms for the clues.

billow / twilled woollen cloth

The longest word in the English language to contain all five vowels in alphabetical order - AEIOU - is abstemiously.

Can you find the longest word to contain all five vowels in reverse alphabetical order - UOIEA ?

What do the following words have in common?

chastening, vindication, revolution, emotionless, praise, brain

Apart from all having abbreviations, what do these phrases have in common?

DC current   LCD display
ISBN number   BASIC code
PIN number   GMT time
NATO organization

The word light forms two words unrelated in meaning, *lightless* and *lightness*, when *less* and *ness* are added. Can you find another 5-letter word which displays this same characteristic, then a 4-letter word, and, finally a 3-letter word?

Many words have dropped out of common usage, but still appear as idioms as part of other words, or with prefixes and suffixes attached. An example of such a word is ruthless, in which the meaning of the little-used word *ruth* is compassion. In the following words and expressions can you spot the fossilized word, and work out its correct meaning as a stand-alone word?

bank teller   swashbuckler   to and fro

Which bracketed word is most similar in meaning to the key word?

INVIOLATE   (animated, envious, alluring, winsome, intact)

If 9L of a C is nine lives of a cat, can you decode the following phrase?

1000 W P in T B

Test One Answer 1
Keep at bay

Test One Answer 2
cellar, arcade, depose, sedate, teaser, ermine, nebula, latest, stance

Test One Answer 3
Esteem, respect

Test One Answer 4
It never rains but it pours.

Test One Answer 5
Manoeuvrable

Test One Answer 6
From head to toe

Test One Answer 7
upstart, parvenu

Test One Answer 8
Sold gold

Test One Answer 9
garotte

Test One Answer 10
cachalot

Test One Answer 11
dank, dry

Test One Answer 12
Small squall

Test One Answer 13
Dispute route

Test One Answer 14
Tipsy gypsy

Test One Answer 15
businessman

Test One Answer 16
TURBOT

Test One Answer 17
Olive, cherry, peach

Test One Answer 18
imprudent, heedless

Test One Answer 19
Chew the cud

Test One Answer 20
Magic, sorcery

Test One Answer 21
circus

Test One Answer 22
Climate

Test One Answer 23
POST

Test One Answer 24
Alphabet

Test One Answer 25
Labrador, Pekingese,

Test One Answer 26
compensate

Test One Answer 27
Pull out all the stops

Test One Answer 28
Hang in there

Test One Answer 29
cruel

Test One Answer 30
(c)   External angle of a building

Test One Answer 31
clothes

Test One Answer 32
Ten, to complete the words carton,
madden and bitten

Test One Answer 33
Their alternate letters spell out a body part:
ear, toe, arm, eye

Test One Answer 34
Marlene Dietrich. DIETRICH becomes RICH DIET

Test One Answer 35
advocate

Test One Answer 36
Short, sweet

Test One Answer 37
NERHO = heron

Test One Answer 38
Charm

Test One Answer 39
Planner – planer

Test One Answer 40
Face to face

Test One Answer 41
Hercules: ash, toe, far, arc, you, pal, hoe, was

Test One Answer 42
Neurotic

Test One Answer 43
cattle,. scathe, locate, Muscat

Test One Answer 44
c.

Test One Answer 45
frame, colour

Test One Answer 46
Old and new: golden, renewal

Test One Answer 47
Act your age

Test One Answer 48
Polar, Koala, Kodiak

Test One Answer 49
Down: all words can be suffixed with RIGHT

Test One Answer 50
Actions speak louder than words

Test Two Answer 1
Once

Test Two Answer 2
Add NSEW to the beginning and WESN to the end
to produce: now, some, eats, win

Test Two Answer 3
See you at ten pm
Ani(see)d, jo(you)sly, b(at)h, an(ten)na,
chi(pm)unk

Test Two Answer 4
ANY ITCHY TIGHT BBC GNAT

Test Two Answer 5
Early – prematurely

Test Two Answer 6
Socrates

Test Two Answer 7
They can all be paired with parts of the body i.e.
green fingers, headway, toenail, armband, leg
work, backbite

Test Two Answer 8
small fortune, same difference, inside out, student
teacher, light heavyweight.

Test Two Answer 9
penury, plenty

Test Two Answer 10
bees

Test Two Answer 11
Billed and build

Test Two Answer 12
pierce, apiece, rapier, magpie

Test Two Answer 13
APRICOT: the last part of capacitor is an anagram
of apricot and the last part of patronage is an
anagram of orange.

Test Two Answer 14
Pawn – prawn

Test Two Answer 15
CANARY

Test Two Answer 16
Stay: all words can be prefixed with main

Test Two Answer 17
Michael Douglas (an anagram of comedial laughs)

Test Two Answer 18
Auld Lang Syne

Test Two Answer 19
Many hands make light work

Test Two Answer 20
Kite, osprey, falcon

Test Two Answer 21
Mister – miser

Test Two Answer 22
Knead, need

Test Two Answer 23
Cliff-face

Test Two Answer 24
13 stripes on the American flag

Test Two Answer 25
SHORT

Test Two Answer 26
Synonyms: toxic, septic
Antonyms: safe

Test Two Answer 27
Arsenal v Chelsea

Test Two Answer 28
C(rat)e

Test Two Answer 29
Quay, ski

Test Two Answer 30
Attention

Test Two Answer 31
Malamute

Test Two Answer 32
obvious, manifest

Test Two Answer 33
Banana, butter, custard

Test Two Answer 34
(c)   Offspring

Test Two Answer 35
O: Take the first three letters in turn added to the last two to spell bat, rat, cat

Test Two Answer 36
Detest

Test Two Answer 37
Mop and scruple
The rest are in pairs where the alternate letters of a seven-letter word spell out a three-letter word i.e. ado – hardtop, rue – trouper, nil – entitle, due – adjured, cap – scrappy

Test Two Answer 38
Wit: witness and witless

Test Two Answer 39
No idea: (no I deer)

Test Two Answer 40
Rubber-stamp

Test Two Answer 41
Add AA, BB, CC, DD, EE, FF, GG, HH to produce aria, blob, chic, deed, ease, fief, gong, high

Test Two Answer 42
Kraal, hobby, accent, cuddle, beech, afford, foggy

Test Two Answer 43
Frogmarch, spatially, snowdrift, overdraft, knowledge, spineless

Test Two Answer 44
Oxford, Orlando, Omsk

Test Two Answer 45
clock, font

Test Two Answer 46
B: to spell back to front in reverse

Test Two Answer 47
Bicycle, coach, train

Test Two Answer 48
Wind

Test Two Answer 49
Partaken: the letters ART are moving up one place in each word.

Test Two Answer 50
Sealskin

Test Three Answer 1
scarlet

Test Three Answer 2
Ephemera

Test Three Answer 3
brightened

Test Three Answer 4
drain man = mandarin
The vegetables are:
cash pin - spinach
take choir - artichoke
spin rap - parsnip
cult tee - lettuce
war secrets - watercress

Test Three Answer 5
Add AULD LANG SYNE to produce cauldron, flange, busyness

Test Three Answer 6
Curtail, curtsey, custard

Test Three Answer 7
TANMO + U = amount

Test Three Answer 8
Throwing a spanner in the works

Test Three Answer 9
lumbago

Test Three Answer 10
wimbrel

Test Three Answer 11
Sincerity, isinglass, insinuate, amusingly, Abyssinia, confusing, Wisconsin

Test Three Answer 12
boorish, civilised

Test Three Answer 13
Flush

Test Three Answer 14
Handle: all words can be prefixed with pan

Test Three Answer 15
Mechanical

Test Three Answer 16
POODLE

Test Three Answer 17
Shoot, chute

Test Three Answer 18
Ring

Test Three Answer 19
spendthrift

Test Three Answer 20
Stardom
star dot minus T plus M

Test Three Answer 21
wide stride
slyer friar
scare Blair
dream team
lacking backing
scan plan
brain drain
grip whip
Llama drama
ration passion

Test Three Answer 22
Scrape – scape

Test Three Answer 23
HAND

Test Three Answer 24
Pick, choose

Test Three Answer 25
Post: apostle, riposte, impostor

Test Three Answer 26
Chemist, fireman, builder

Test Three Answer 27
random,. orange, errant, outran

Test Three Answer 28
Synonyms: enthralled, agog
Antonym: apathetic

Test Three Answer 29
Animals: marzi(pan, da)hlia, oxi(de, er)ror,
ser(mon, key)note, bron(ze, bra)zen,
alka(li, on)ion, se(ll, ama)lgam

Test Three Answer 30
Soc(key)e

Test Three Answer 31
Niagara, O roar again

Test Three Answer 32
(a)   Gout

Test Three Answer 33
LORMTA = mortal

Test Three Answer 34
look a gift horse in the mouth

Test Three Answer 35
Ghost-writer, prize-winner, screw-driver, first-
string, candle-stick, mortar-board, corner-stone,
school-child

Test Three Answer 36
post, stop, spot, tops, pots, opts

Test Three Answer 37
persevere, maintain

Test Three Answer 38
Presence, presents

Test Three Answer 39
Somnambulate (mutable moans)

Test Three Answer 40
Synonyms: evasive, circuitous
Antonym: direct

Test Three Answer 41
odd one out
on the boil
call the tune
cut and dried
in deep water
keep an eye out
other fish to fry
lay down the law
a miss is as good as a mile
pass the buck

Test Three Answer 42
poverty

Test Three Answer 43
tide, waves

Test Three Answer 44
Arnold Schwarzenegger
(anagram: crazed leghorn gnawers)

Test Three Answer 45
Punster – punter

Test Three Answer 46
Verbose and observe

Test Three Answer 47
Point

Test Three Answer 48
Madeleine : to give hum, sea, nod, foe, owl, toe, ski, ran, cue

Test Three Answer 49
T(rifle)r

Test Three Answer 50
dismay

Test Four Answer 1
Fundamental

Test Four Answer 2
star, stare, stargaze, starlet, starry-eyed, stardom.

Test Four Answer 3
Oceanic, pelagic

Test Four Answer 4
JOLLY: each letter moves forward the same number of places in the alphabet.

Test Four Answer 5
Debonair

Test Four Answer 6
Dust

Test Four Answer 7
You are never too old to learn

Test Four Answer 8
lock, stock, barrel

Test Four Answer 9
Fly: all words can be suffixed with weight

Test Four Answer 10
Dennis and Edna sinned

Test Four Answer 11
docile

Test Four Answer 12
Get – procure

Test Four Answer 13
larceny, honesty

Test Four Answer 14
IGUANA

Test Four Answer 15
Lie in wait

Test Four Answer 16
Add I, V, X, C, D, M (Roman numerals) to produce stair, carve, latex, bract, medal, chomp

Test Four Answer 17
Bogus – counterfeit

Test Four Answer 18
too many cooks spoil the broth
many hands make light work
(mark my shaking hand-towel)

Test Four Answer 19
CAN<u>DID</u> CAMERA

Test Four Answer 20
succour, remedy

Test Four Answer 21
b

Test Four Answer 22
feet

Test Four Answer 23
exit

Test Four Answer 24
Waywardly

Test Four Answer 25
one swallow doesn't make a summer

Test Four Answer 26
Moon: all words in the first column can
be prefixed with BLUE and in the second
column the words can be prefixed with RED

Test Four Answer 27
Tube

Test Four Answer 28
Synonyms: protect, conserve
Antonym: destroy

Test Four Answer 29
CAR

Test Four Answer 30
(c)   Relating to a fish

Test Four Answer 31
train, educate, instruct, coach

Test Four Answer 32
substance

Test Four Answer 33
Side – line – up – date – palm – tree – top – side

Test Four Answer 34
bed of nails

Test Four Answer 35
All sea going vessels - dhow, raft,
sloop, brig, punt, barge, canoe

Test Four Answer 36
penitent – sorry, similar - alike
enthusiast – fan, detailed - exact
proficient – able, erstwhile - late

Test Four Answer 37
Cha(pea)u

Test Four Answer 38
MINERAL (ENIGMA) KINGDOM
ASTAIRE (ANSWER) TINWARE
  3 1 6   1 23 45 6   2 4 5

Test Four Answer 39
Shard

Test Four Answer 40
tape/pert, side/desk, most/star, meal/ally

8 - letter word : pedestal

Test Four Answer 41

acronym
second ba**ll**et
centre of Chi**c**ago
sixth forme**r**
first **o**ffender
non-starter
satisfactor**y** conclusion
botto**m** end

Test Four Answer 42

They can be prefixed with P to form another
word: plate, please, padded, praise, putter

Test Four Answer 43

i) imagination, ii) incomprehensibility,
iii) gravitation, iv) persistent, v) mysterious

Test Four Answer 44

wings, pilot

Test Four Answer 45

Deep

Test Four Answer 46

Apricot, plum, grape

Test Four Answer 47

Rainbow

Test Four Answer 48

Rate

Test Four Answer 49

Carp, dace, pike, trout

Test Four Answer 50

Pine – pint – paint – saint – stint – stink – sink –
sin – pin – pine

Test Five Answer 1

Diabolical (anagram: bold Alicia)

Test Five Answer 2

tall, dark, handsome

Test Five Answer 3

lassitude

Test Five Answer 4

Cyan, fawn, gold, ruby, black, coral, sable

Test Five Answer 5

PECOLU = couple

Test Five Answer 6

Stage – sage

Test Five Answer 7

ZZ: work from bottom line to top in turn
and vice versa to spell MONKEY PUZZLE

Test Five Answer 8

Bell

Test Five Answer 9

i) leading man, ii) sleep tight, iii) odd one out,
iv) not a hope

Test Five Answer 10

support, hinder

Test Five Answer 11

i) graceful (Gulf race), ii) bibliographer (glib hair
probe), iii) righteousness (resting houses), iv)
transship (spin trash)

Test Five Answer 12

i. great ape   grey tape
ii. known ocean no notion

Test Five Answer 13
Rapier, repair

Test Five Answer 14
LUPINE

Test Five Answer 15
Motiveless, resolvable, unresolved

Test Five Answer 16
Paint – brush – off – duty – free – will –
power – house – coat

Test Five Answer 17
Now Ned I am a maiden nun,
Ned I am a maiden won

Test Five Answer 18
senile felines, name no one man,
never odd or even

Test Five Answer 19
north polar

Test Five Answer 20
Spelunker

Test Five Answer 21
peridot and emerald

Test Five Answer 22
Metropolitan

Test Five Answer 23
Let them eat cake

Test Five Answer 24
CON

Test Five Answer 25
Mean

Test Five Answer 26
Arcane: the recognised initials for the three states
are AR, CA, NE

Test Five Answer 27
marquess

Test Five Answer 28
upholder

Test Five Answer 29
(b)   Intoxicating drink

Test Five Answer 30
fifteen, thirty five, seventy, eighty one, ninety
three, three hundred, eight thousand, forty million

Test Five Answer 31
slovenly, slack

Test Five Answer 32
indisposed, sustenance, apostate, gourmet,
stereotype, espionage, garrulous

Test Five Answer 33
c

Test Five Answer 34
TBOAL = bloat

Test Five Answer 35
astuteness

Test Five Answer 36
Thomas Alva Edison (anagram:
lavish anode atoms)

Test Five Answer 37
now here – nowhere

Test Five Answer 38

Add a, e, i, o, u to produce chain, beacon, biased, coat, statue

Test Five Answer 39

guitar

Test Five Answer 40

months, days

Test Five Answer 41

emerald, ruby, topaz
grape, apple, pear
horse, elephant, lion

Test Five Answer 42

saw nothing = Washington
The countries are:
and ionise = Indonesia
lizard newts = Switzerland
big Laura = Bulgaria
regain tan = Argentina

Test Five Answer 43

Tasmanian possum, European bison, bactrian camel, Pyrenean mountain dog, horseshoe bat, Patagonian cavy, sealyham terrier, Christmas beetle

Test Five Answer 44

wind

Test Five Answer 45

Friday, island, Selkirk, maroon

The link is Robinson Crusoe (Alexander Selkirk was the real-life mariner on whose life Robinson Crusoe was based)

Test Five Answer 46

a) Barbra Streisand

b) Ferdinand Magellan
c) Andre Agassi
d) Amelia Earhart

Test Five Answer 47

Answer word: continued; unnoticed (anagram), resumed (synonym), ended (antonym)
Answer word: glisten; singlet (anagram), shimmer (synonym), fade (antonym)
Answer word: considerate; desecration (anagram), thoughtful (synonym), negligent (antonym)

Test Five Answer 48

Truth will out

Test Five Answer 49

Innocent

Test Five Answer 50

Geisha, hassle, length, thirst, stooge

Test Six Answer 1

Snug & raw was I ere I saw war & guns

Test Six Answer 2

hostility

Test Six Answer 3

cushions

Test Six Answer 4

The letters AB. Anne Boleyn, aurora borealis, atom bomb, Ali Baba, aneroid barometer

Test Six Answer 5

Telephone, computer, calendar

Test Six Answer 6

Bacon and egg (BA = degree, con = hoodwink, intellectually ahead = egg head)

Test Six Answer 7
Home from home

Test Six Answer 8
bumpkin

Test Six Answer 9
Take to task, again and again, whole wide world, tell the time

Test Six Answer 10
impracticable

Test Six Answer 11
left, right, centre

Test Six Answer 12
loth, willing

Test Six Answer 13
kipper and salmon

Test Six Answer 14
Ponytail

Test Six Answer 15
BANANA

Test Six Answer 16
S(pear)mint

Test Six Answer 17
Synonyms: severe, stringent
Antonym: flexible

Test Six Answer 18
Guest, guessed

Test Six Answer 19
secure, rebuke, kennel, elapse

Test Six Answer 20
delightful

Test Six Answer 21
Way off beam

Test Six Answer 22
Damned, demand

Test Six Answer 23
Rain: brainy, drained, sprained, moraine, drainage

Test Six Answer 24
Congratulations

Test Six Answer 25
labyrinth

Test Six Answer 26
BAR

Test Six Answer 27
beat

Test Six Answer 28
Loaves, overlaps, cloves, sloven or novels

Test Six Answer 29
fortify, reinforce

Test Six Answer 30
Roulette

Test Six Answer 31
(a)   Soldier

Test Six Answer 32
Add HIT THE HAY to produce white, bother, sashayed

Test Six Answer 33
The Old Curiosity Shop (anagram:
the lousy chiropodist)

Test Six Answer 34
Less

Test Six Answer 35
You can talk

Test Six Answer 36
Fourteen, seventeen, twenty-one

Test Six Answer 37
Second chance. The rest all repeat a pair
of letters in each word, e.g. postage stamp

Test Six Answer 38
high seas

Test Six Answer 39
Sore, Eros

Test Six Answer 40
Balladeer, withering, postilion, yellowish,
cellulose

Test Six Answer 41
Sauce – impudence

Test Six Answer 42
Pupils slip up

Test Six Answer 43
Chic, squeak

Test Six Answer 44
Mitzi and Kathleen. The initial letters of the
other girl's spell SANTA CLAUS

Test Six Answer 45
work hard

Test Six Answer 46
Add WELL DONE to produce dwelling, abandoned

Test Six Answer 47
binary – brainy

Test Six Answer 48
shaven raven

Test Six Answer 49
Atlas. The symbols for the elements are at, la, s

Test Six Answer 50
Finger - nail – polish – off – hand

Test Seven Answer 1
Go over the top

Test Seven Answer 2
Canada and Greece

Test Seven Answer 3
Answer word: resign; singer (anagram), quit
(synonym), enlist (antonym)
Answer word: nadir; drain (anagram), base
(synonym), top (antonym)
Answer word: fluster; restful (anagram), agitate
(synonym), placate (antonym)

Test Seven Answer 4
Sigmund Freud

Test Seven Answer 5
Sir Humphrey Davy

Test Seven Answer 6
Hand: all words can be prefixed with short

Test Seven Answer 7
Probe – investigate

Test Seven Answer 8
hung, drawn, quartered

Test Seven Answer 9
reject

Test Seven Answer 10
boorish, civil

Test Seven Answer 11
Cause – cayuse

Test Seven Answer 12
Sums are not set as a test on Erasmus

Test Seven Answer 13
ALMOND

Test Seven Answer 14
Trees: plane, pear, pine, palm, date

Test Seven Answer 15
Base

Test Seven Answer 16
Chink

Test Seven Answer 17
cloud : the vowels appear in repeated
sequence: a, e, i, o, u

Test Seven Answer 18
Agatha: the sequence of letters a, b, c, d, e, f, g, h
appear in the same position in each of the words.

Test Seven Answer 19
They all have a mountainous link:

lem(ur al)cove Ural
sc(alp s)nake Alps
c(rock y)ield Rocky
st(and es)py Andes

Test Seven Answer 20
hold

Test Seven Answer 21
Skewer, spatula, cruet

Test Seven Answer 22
Rifle, riffle

Test Seven Answer 23
They all become creatures with the addition of a
single letter: salmon, tiger, monkey, snail

Test Seven Answer 24
Later – latter

Test Seven Answer 25
FOOT

Test Seven Answer 26
Kennel – kernel

Test Seven Answer 27
Ruder – rudder

Test Seven Answer 28
balalaika

Test Seven Answer 29
MIG(RAIN)E

Test Seven Answer 30
Causal, casual

Test Seven Answer 31
thirty seven, forty six, fifty one

Test Seven Answer 32
(c)   Self evident truth

Test Seven Answer 33
Synonyms: unaware, oblivious
Antonym: attentive

Test Seven Answer 34
Big bang, peace pipe, white wine, think tank, due date, fossil fuel, lady luck

Test Seven Answer 35
Bad hair day

Test Seven Answer 36
hallowed, revered

Test Seven Answer 37
Count, tally

Test Seven Answer 38
Trap

Test Seven Answer 39
Lamb – lamp – camp – damp – dame – Dane – lane – line – lime – lame – lamb

Test Seven Answer 40
a) Konrad Adenauer
b) Enrico Caruso
c) George Armstrong Custer
d) Rafael Sabatini

Test Seven Answer 41
Maps – spam, stressed – desserts, repaid – diaper

Test Seven Answer 42
pitiable

Test Seven Answer 43
Pseudonym

Test Seven Answer 44
grounds

Test Seven Answer 45
six lines, six sides

Test Seven Answer 46
Out of step

Test Seven Answer 47
Scoundrel

Test Seven Answer 48
Mucilage

Test Seven Answer 49
Barbershop-quartet

Test Seven Answer 50
Once: conceal, conceit, concede

Test Eight Answer 1
hook, line, sinker

Test Eight Answer 2
Storm

Test Eight Answer 3
They can all be typed on the middle row of a QWERTY keyboard (asdfghjkl)

Test Eight Answer 4
AF(FORD)ABLE

Test Eight Answer 5
Ha-ha, hi-fi, re-do

Test Eight Answer 6
Cro(cod)ile

Test Eight Answer 7
Camel-hair, spread-eagle

Test Eight Answer 8
Hammock (comma)

Test Eight Answer 9
They all contain countries:
ma(china)tion, for(mali)ty, in(cuba)te,
s(chad)enfreude

Test Eight Answer 10
Nurse, I spy gypsies run

Test Eight Answer 11
Far-reaching

Test Eight Answer 12
foyer

Test Eight Answer 13
swamp, subside

Test Eight Answer 14
Feasible

Test Eight Answer 15
CATTLE

Test Eight Answer 16
Lark

Test Eight Answer 17
crater-cater

Test Eight Answer 18
Absent without leave

Test Eight Answer 19
a. gull – bull, b. owl – fowl, c. eider – elder

Test Eight Answer 20
S(AUNT)ER

Test Eight Answer 21
Nostradamus

Test Eight Answer 22
sedated, effigy, sublimely, appeared,
impeachment, bugling

Test Eight Answer 23
mouse, trap, door, step, father, land, mark,
time, out, fox, hole

Test Eight Answer 24
UNDER

Test Eight Answer 25
regiment
The rest are anagram pairs - intoxicate/excitation,
cheat/teach, creation/reaction,
statement/testament, senator/treason,
observe/verbose, demand/madden

Test Eight Answer 26
cabal, clique

Test Eight Answer 27
Preface – introduction

Test Eight Answer 28
cock and bull
cat and dog
cut and run

Test Eight Answer 29
eat humble pie, none the wiser,
take to heart

Test Eight Answer 30
(d)　　　Sea cucumber

Test Eight Answer 31
the difficult is easy and the impossible is
a little bit harder

Test Eight Answer 32
pig, wig, wag, way, say, sty

Test Eight Answer 33
fir, oak, ash

Test Eight Answer 34
Amiably, ammonia, amongst

Test Eight Answer 35
rash

Test Eight Answer 36
scared – sacred

Test Eight Answer 37
Fire: quick fire, fireside, fire brand, crossfire

Test Eight Answer 38
Maiden, median

Test Eight Answer 39
Spherical

Test Eight Answer 40
P(IRAN)HA

Test Eight Answer 41
tug rug

Test Eight Answer 42
Tomorrow

Test Eight Answer 43
One step forwards, two steps back

Test Eight Answer 44
For better or for worse

Test Eight Answer 45
Sincerely, isinglass, disinfect, tipsiness
Blessings, limousine, Wisconsin

Test Eight Answer 46
rook, bishop

Test Eight Answer 47
woebegone, illgotten, pantryman, pentagram,
redevelop, warrantor

Test Eight Answer 48
beachcomber (her BBC cameo)
circumnavigate (cure TV magician)
lighthouse (eighth soul)
downstream (new stardom)
undercurrent (cut red runner)

Test Eight Answer 49
The Prodigal Son, it contains the word *also*, while
all the others contain the word *and*.

The Americ**an D**ream
The Gr**and** Canyon
A Little Engl**and**er
The Prodig**al So**n
A Ne**and**erthal Man
The Ten Comm**and**ments

Test Eight Answer 50
selling dwelling

Test Nine Answer 1
Splendid, admirable, remarkable, sublime

Test Nine Answer 2
bell, book, candle

Test Nine Answer 3
Intricately (anagram: tiny article)

Test Nine Answer 4
Four of the words must be reversed before pairing them with the remaining four words to produce: bingo, warrant, torrent, pardon

Test Nine Answer 5
dottrel

Test Nine Answer 6
Wind

Test Nine Answer 7
Samantha, Selina, Sandra

Test Nine Answer 8
Plane mayday

Test Nine Answer 9
Ink: each word commences with the letter which comes two places in the alphabet after the last letter of the previous word, for example, aquatic (d) earwig

Test Nine Answer 10
teak, pear, plane

Test Nine Answer 11
dreamy, practical

Test Nine Answer 12
Coin-operated

Test Nine Answer 13
MARROW

Test Nine Answer 14
Rocky

Test Nine Answer 15
Cross-section

Test Nine Answer 16
Sir, I demand, I am a maid named Iris

Test Nine Answer 17
Answer word: education; cautioned (anagram), learning (synonym), illiteracy (antonym)
Answer word: lament; mental (anagram), bewail (synonym), rejoice (antonym)
Answer word: dearth; thread (anagram), insufficiency (synonym), abundance (antonym)

Test Nine Answer 18
Nevada

Test Nine Answer 19
hue and cry, fun and games, pen and ink

Test Nine Answer 20
so-so, to-do, yo-yo

Test Nine Answer 21
Under lock and key

Test Nine Answer 22
Add ODD ONE OUT to produce shoddy, honest, south

Test Nine Answer 23
PAR

Test Nine Answer 24
Bene(vole)nce

Test Nine Answer 25
War: wart, wary, warp, ware, ward

Test Nine Answer 26
Din – pandemonium

Test Nine Answer 27
T P G S W S M D F
E A E K A E A U I
A L L I G A T O R

Test Nine Answer 28
Receptionist, bricklayer, kennelmaid

Test Nine Answer 29
faculty, capacity

Test Nine Answer 30
They can all be prefixed by relatives:
Aunt Sally, Uncle Sam, Mother Goose, Father Time,
Granny knot, Grandfather clock

Test Nine Answer 31
(d)   Card game

Test Nine Answer 32
slower mower

Test Nine Answer 33
ABCD: abdicate

Test Nine Answer 34
Lively, torpid

Test Nine Answer 35
SSSSSS + EEEELNN = senselessness

Test Nine Answer 36
Ascertain, desiccate, increased

Test Nine Answer 37
war and peace, at long last, in good shape

Test Nine Answer 38
Print – pint

Test Nine Answer 39
wheels, rails

Test Nine Answer 40
hatter, hammer

Test Nine Answer 41
RSTU: custard

Test Nine Answer 42
Plough, furrow

Test Nine Answer 43
GGG + AELU = luggage

Test Nine Answer 44
buggy, buddy

Test Nine Answer 45
hand, hard, lard, lord, ford, fort, foot

Test Nine Answer 46
Foal, pony, stallion

Test Nine Answer 47
Roomy moor

Test Nine Answer 48
Hoarse – horse

Test Nine Answer 49
Vast, abundant, significant, mammoth,
superior, enormous, immense
Anagram = massive

Test Nine Answer 50
To err is human to forgive divine

Test Ten Answer 1
respect

Test Ten Answer 2
Paint

Test Ten Answer 3
G
So that the alternate letters spell
London, England

Test Ten Answer 4
charming

Test Ten Answer 5
rag, tag, bobtail

Test Ten Answer 6
Revolt – insurrection

Test Ten Answer 7
81 squares in a Sudoku puzzle

Test Ten Answer 8
Attest, certify

Test Ten Answer 9
Kay, a red nude peeped under a yak

Test Ten Answer 10
inspire, dishearten

Test Ten Answer 11
The year dot

Test Ten Answer 12
Add CUT AND RUN to produce scuttle, bandit,
crunch

Test Ten Answer 13
sherry

Test Ten Answer 14
Slack jack

Test Ten Answer 15
Act your age

Test Ten Answer 16
FORGER

Test Ten Answer 17
Cash point (# = hash (cash) . = point)

Test Ten Answer 18
Trapezium

Test Ten Answer 19
up and down, wheeling and dealing,
Adam and Eve

Test Ten Answer 20
glib, slippery

Test Ten Answer 21
Add ANY OLD HOW to produce canyon, golden,
shower

Test Ten Answer 22
Fifty-fifty

Test Ten Answer 23
Manicurist, journalist, underwriter

Test Ten Answer 24
higher choir

Test Ten Answer 25
fall into place, no great shakes, seven year itch

Test Ten Answer 26
OVER

Test Ten Answer 27
tree

Test Ten Answer 28
The meek shall inherit the earth

Test Ten Answer 29
Put a brave face on it

Test Ten Answer 30
solitaire, bridge, poker

Test Ten Answer 31
(c)   Badger

Test Ten Answer 32
Synonyms: soothe, pacify
Antonym: irritate

Test Ten Answer 33
Overslept, revulsion, voiceless, insolvable, loveliness

Test Ten Answer 34
FGHI: goldfish

Test Ten Answer 35
The worse for wear.

Test Ten Answer 36
God save the King

Test Ten Answer 37
doily

Test Ten Answer 38
clique

Test Ten Answer 39
Court-martial

Test Ten Answer 40
coat, hair

Test Ten Answer 41
dark park

Test Ten Answer 42
Magazine

Test Ten Answer 43
They are all anagrams of world capitals:
Nassau, Manila, Quito, Athens

Test Ten Answer 44
Spectacular
Unbelievable
Phenomenal
Excellent
Remarkable
Breathtaking
(SUPERB)

Test Ten Answer 45
more, lore, lose, loss, less

Test Ten Answer 46
Cut down to size and take down a peg or two

Test Ten Answer 47
They all contain four consecutive letters of the alphabet:
Strategi(c def)ence initiative, Fi(lm no)ir, Genus tha(mnop)hilus, Designe(r stu)bble

Test Ten Answer 48
Higher choir

Test Ten Answer 49
Barking up the wrong tree

Test Ten Answer 50
rebellious

Test Eleven Answer 1
musket

Test Eleven Answer 2
Toronto, Ostend, Eindhoven, Avignon, Madras, Nagasaki, Limerick, Rotterdam
Anagram: Montreal

Test Eleven Answer 3
Add FOCAL POINT to produce bifocals, appointee

Test Eleven Answer 4
Add NEW FOR OLD to produce sinewy, afford, golden

Test Eleven Answer 5
Writhe, write

Test Eleven Answer 6
XYZ = law

lawyer, clawed, Malawi, outlaw

Test Eleven Answer 7
Winter wonderland (win, won)

Test Eleven Answer 8
stars and stripes, by and large, cat and mouse

Test Eleven Answer 9
shoesmith

Test Eleven Answer 10
Machinate

Test Eleven Answer 11
Raider – rider

Test Eleven Answer 12
inviolate, corrupt

Test Eleven Answer 13
The pen is mightier than the sword

Test Eleven Answer 14
MOSAIC

Test Eleven Answer 15
Anthropologist, librarian, coastguard, elocutionist

Test Eleven Answer 16
Synonyms: erudite, learned
Antonym: illiterate

Test Eleven Answer 17
endure, remote, teacup, upbeat, attach, chosen

Test Eleven Answer 18
Rescue – liberate

Test Eleven Answer 19
Star: custard, mustard, upstart, dastard

Test Eleven Answer 20
shake, rattle, roll

Test Eleven Answer 21
Doc, note, I dissent, a fast never prevents
a fatness I diet on cod.

Test Eleven Answer 22
Sporting, unfair

Test Eleven Answer 23
ICE
ACE
ATE
SKATER

Test Eleven Answer 24
jolly polly

Test Eleven Answer 25
UNDER

Test Eleven Answer 26
Synonyms: recruit, enrol
Antonym: dismiss

Test Eleven Answer 27
insatiable, rapacious

Test Eleven Answer 28
Soared, sword

Test Eleven Answer 29
DEFG: glorified

Test Eleven Answer 30
score more

Test Eleven Answer 31
C(abba)ge

Test Eleven Answer 32
(c)   Bell tower

Test Eleven Answer 33
straight

Test Eleven Answer 34
Mite, might

Test Eleven Answer 35
Tractor

Test Eleven Answer 36
Soccer rocker

Test Eleven Answer 37
Entrance and entrance

Test Eleven Answer 38
London and linden

Test Eleven Answer 39
boat, wheel

Test Eleven Answer 40
Pipe

Test Eleven Answer 41
Bankruptcy

Test Eleven Answer 42
Recede, ebb, retreat

Test Eleven Answer 43
Manner, aspect

Test Eleven Answer 44
desecrated

Test Eleven Answer 45
grip whip

Test Eleven Answer 46
d

Test Eleven Answer 47
Testator

Test Eleven Answer 48
visitor, caller, guest

Test Eleven Answer 49
An ace in the hole

Test Eleven Answer 50
FLOG RANDY = dragonfly

The cheeses are camembert (crab met me), mozzarella (loam razzle) and parmesan (smear pan)

Test Twelve Answer 1
Soprano: each word begins with the initials of the musical tonic scale in order:
do, re, mi, fa, sol, la, ti, do

Test Twelve Answer 2
ma(gnu)m

Test Twelve Answer 3
I moved the tome to me

Test Twelve Answer 4
AUTHORITY - throaty
BANDWAGON – abandon

Test Twelve Answer 5
basset

Test Twelve Answer 6
0 degrees latitude of the equator

Test Twelve Answer 7
Liberia/Sudan

Test Twelve Answer 8
bloom, lies

Test Twelve Answer 9
Athos, Porthos, Aramis (the Three Musketeers)

Test Twelve Answer 10
manacle

Test Twelve Answer 11
Plush display

Test Twelve Answer 12
malice, goodwill

Test Twelve Answer 13
CLOUDY

Test Twelve Answer 14
demand remand

Test Twelve Answer 15
Afar: the second letters are in the sequence
a, b, c, d, e, f

Test Twelve Answer 16
Adjective (anagram: jive cadet)

Test Twelve Answer 17
come clean
do or die

Test Twelve Answer 18
Ti(moth)y

Test Twelve Answer 19
na(nose)econd

Test Twelve Answer 20
ABCDE: barricade

Test Twelve Answer 21
knave – nave

Test Twelve Answer 22
RID: hatred and ridden

Test Twelve Answer 23
DILLTU + EFGH = delightful

Test Twelve Answer 24
MOON

Test Twelve Answer 25
Purify, befoul

Test Twelve Answer 26
They all require one letter adding to
the end to produce girls' names:
Hope, Beth, Mary, Tina, Ruby and Hazel.

Test Twelve Answer 27
(a)   Wicker covered bottle

Test Twelve Answer 28
'Tis Ivan on a visit

Test Twelve Answer 29
Glorified

Test Twelve Answer 30
old gold

Test Twelve Answer 31
legs, upholstery

Test Twelve Answer 32
5 rings on the Olympic flag

Test Twelve Answer 33
catacomb - tomb
container - can/tin
curtail - cut

Test Twelve Answer 34
AF(FORD)ABLE

Test Twelve Answer 35
Drawback, asset

Test Twelve Answer 36
Tonga/Libya = Italy/Gabon

Test Twelve Answer 37
lorikeet

Test Twelve Answer 38
Age

Test Twelve Answer 39
gal(leo)n

Test Twelve Answer 40
tended net

Test Twelve Answer 41
P(IRAN)HA

Test Twelve Answer 42
operate, perform

Test Twelve Answer 43
9 planets in the solar system

Test Twelve Answer 44
Spruce

Test Twelve Answer 45
rise to vote sir

Test Twelve Answer 46
intelligence test : each begins with the
middle two letters of the phrase above.

Test Twelve Answer 47
blessed
cursed

Test Twelve Answer 48
Nomenclature (anagram: neater column)

Test Twelve Answer 49
grill Will

Test Twelve Answer 50
deceased - dead
deliberate - debate
encourage - urge

Test Thirteen Answer 1
E R
Read across each line including the small case
letters to spell out the words: arable, candle,
eyeful, gopher

Test Thirteen Answer 2
Camp: camper, campus, camphor

Test Thirteen Answer 3
Let us pray

Test Thirteen Answer 4
Add COME INTO PLAY to produce newcomer,
badminton, ballplayer

Test Thirteen Answer 5
altering, relating, triangle, alerting, integral

Test Thirteen Answer 6
Importance

Test Thirteen Answer 7
c(oven)ant

Test Thirteen Answer 8
Amen: lament, filament, tameness

Test Thirteen Answer 9
starve

Test Thirteen Answer 10
Shadrach, Meshach, Abednego

Test Thirteen Answer 11
odorous, malodorous

Test Thirteen Answer 12
ocean motion

Test Thirteen Answer 13
Se(dime)nt

Test Thirteen Answer 14
sphere

Test Thirteen Answer 15
A(NERO)ID

Test Thirteen Answer 16
BERLIN

Test Thirteen Answer 17
Synonyms: composed, serene
Antonym: agitated

Test Thirteen Answer 18
Reverse each set of three letters to reveal the
phrase Make haste slowly.

Test Thirteen Answer 19
A dog! A panic in a pagoda

Test Thirteen Answer 20
opaque

Test Thirteen Answer 21
LMNOP: complain

Test Thirteen Answer 22
TILAEN = entail

Test Thirteen Answer 23
It was the season for the sea son.

Test Thirteen Answer 24
repulsive, distasteful

Test Thirteen Answer 25
s(harp s)hooter

Test Thirteen Answer 26
STAR

Test Thirteen Answer 27
jingle jangle

Test Thirteen Answer 28
(a)   Tail-less rodent

Test Thirteen Answer 29
Amazon and Thames

Test Thirteen Answer 30
17 syllables in a Haiku

Test Thirteen Answer 31
CONUNDRUM - corundum
DIPLOMACY - olympiad

Test Thirteen Answer 32
star comedy: democrats

Test Thirteen Answer 33
evacuate - vacate
exist - is
fabrication - fiction

Test Thirteen Answer 34
top spot

Test Thirteen Answer 35
Mali/Qatar = Iraq/Malta

Test Thirteen Answer 36
sensible

Test Thirteen Answer 37
Pack – the chemical symbols are pa = Pascal,
c = Coulomb, k = Kelvin

Test Thirteen Answer 38
goal posts, pitch

Test Thirteen Answer 39
calmness

Test Thirteen Answer 40
Wolf herd

Test Thirteen Answer 41
ge(nero)us

Test Thirteen Answer 42
abnormal

Test Thirteen Answer 43
The staff were managing with the man aging.

Test Thirteen Answer 44
shrewd nude

Test Thirteen Answer 45
Intrepid

Test Thirteen Answer 46
Looking back over the years

Test Thirteen Answer 47
hit or miss
ill at ease

Test Thirteen Answer 48
20 years slept by Rip Van Winkle.

Test Thirteen Answer 49
facade - face
hostelry - hotel
illuminated - lit

Test Thirteen Answer 50
Beloves, novelist, livestock

Test Fourteen Answer 1
The Andes

Test Fourteen Answer 2
plain

Test Fourteen Answer 3
Add TIME WILL TELL to produce untimely, swilled, patella

Test Fourteen Answer 4
1 good turn deserves another

Test Fourteen Answer 5
stun nuts

Test Fourteen Answer 6
pretty ditty

Test Fourteen Answer 7
fish

Test Fourteen Answer 8
ROD, ROT, POT, PIT, PISTON

Test Fourteen Answer 9
Jackpot

Test Fourteen Answer 10
broad minded, bigoted

Test Fourteen Answer 11
Her ring was swallowed by the herring.

Test Fourteen Answer 12
nom de (plum)e

Test Fourteen Answer 13
allow

Test Fourteen Answer 14
EFGHI: freighter

Test Fourteen Answer 15
BURGER

Test Fourteen Answer 16
I have too many irons in the fire

Test Fourteen Answer 17
joviality – joy, market – mart,
matches - mates

Test Fourteen Answer 18
never even

Test Fourteen Answer 19
ECONOMIST - emotions
FREQUENCY - fencer

Test Fourteen Answer 20
An(atom)y

Test Fourteen Answer 21
2 heads are better than one

Test Fourteen Answer 22
mixed emotions (fear, anger, joy)

Test Fourteen Answer 23
all in a day's work

Test Fourteen Answer 24
not so Boston

Test Fourteen Answer 25
SIDE

Test Fourteen Answer 26
corn on the cob

Test Fourteen Answer 27
threadbare, to give: moth/thin, tire/rest, toad/adze, tuba/bale, more/reed

Test Fourteen Answer 28
Quality, quartet, quacked

Test Fourteen Answer 29
long prong

Test Fourteen Answer 30
worship

Test Fourteen Answer 31
occasional, infrequent

Test Fourteen Answer 32
32 capsules on the London Eye

Test Fourteen Answer 33
(b)   Bullet

Test Fourteen Answer 34
stop spots

Test Fourteen Answer 35
name no one man

Test Fourteen Answer 36
lend a hand
live in sin

Test Fourteen Answer 37
Women board

Test Fourteen Answer 38
dead or alive

Test Fourteen Answer 39
observe - see
pantaloons - pants
perambulate - r/amble

Test Fourteen Answer 40
pilot – plot

Test Fourteen Answer 41
12 pairs of ribs in the human body

Test Fourteen Answer 42

PYX	a type of chest
LAM	to beat soundly or thrash
ADZ	a carpenter's tool
YAW	an erratic diversion from an intended course
OKA	South American wood
NIM	a game in which matchsticks are arranged in rows
WAW	the sixth letter of the Hebrew alphabet

OLM	a European cave-dwelling salamander
RYA	a shag rug traditionally made in Sweden
DAG	the unbranched antler of a young deer
SOU	an old French copper coin

Test Fourteen Answer 43
c(lima)x

Test Fourteen Answer 44
GARDENING - deranging
HUMILIATE - lithium

Test Fourteen Answer 45
quaint saint

Test Fourteen Answer 46
Chaos – pandemonium

Test Fourteen Answer 47
Effulgent

Test Fourteen Answer 48
eat humble pie

Test Fourteen Answer 49
Full-length

Test Fourteen Answer 50
Pitch

Test Fifteen Answer 1
temperate

Test Fifteen Answer 2
Add WITH OPEN ARMS to produce
wherewithal, propensity, farmstead

Test Fifteen Answer 3
LMNOP: clampdown

Test Fifteen Answer 4
The gravest ones moved the gravestones

Test Fifteen Answer 5
change of venue

Test Fifteen Answer 6
18 holes on a golf course

Test Fifteen Answer 7
man in the moon

Test Fifteen Answer 8
cut - lacerate

Test Fifteen Answer 9
onerous, light

Test Fifteen Answer 10
Pine – spinet

Test Fifteen Answer 11
IMPUDENCE - endemic
JUXTAPOSE - sexpot

Test Fifteen Answer 12
forest florist

Test Fifteen Answer 13
regal lager

Test Fifteen Answer 14
MINUET

Test Fifteen Answer 15
3 men in a boat by Jerome K Jerome

Test Fifteen Answer 16
Rubens

Test Fifteen Answer 17
in(cuba)tor

Test Fifteen Answer 18
perimeter - rim
prattle - prate
precipitation - rain

Test Fifteen Answer 19
Arrange them in pairs so that they share
the first and last letters.

Lever – rage, Libra – Arian, arch – hives,
front – tier, arm – mature, port – table

After deleting one of the common letters the
following words are produced: leverage,
librarian, archives, frontier, armature, portable.

Test Fifteen Answer 20
men at arms
neon light

Test Fifteen Answer 21
never odd or even

Test Fifteen Answer 22
11 lords a leaping in the Twelve Days of Christmas

Test Fifteen Answer 23
KISSOGRAM - orgasms
LAUGHABLE - haulage

Test Fifteen Answer 24
bankruptcies
considerably
malnourished
ambidextrous
discountable

None of the words repeats a letter.

Test Fifteen Answer 25
inscribe, imprint

Test Fifteen Answer 26
Ruby, pearl, sapphire

Test Fifteen Answer 27
Matisse

Test Fifteen Answer 28
strait / straight

Test Fifteen Answer 29
Cross – country – music – box – car – jack –
knife – point – out – door – key – word

Test Fifteen Answer 30
(b)   Pope's letter

Test Fifteen Answer 31
bright night

Test Fifteen Answer 32
AFGI + LMNO = flamingo

Test Fifteen Answer 33
reindeer, nyala, opossum, gorilla, koala,
onager, antelope, armadillo

Anagram: kangaroo

Test Fifteen Answer 34
INTER

Test Fifteen Answer 35
Hill – chilly

Test Fifteen Answer 36
com(paris)on

Test Fifteen Answer 37
Dennis sinned

Test Fifteen Answer 38
4 United States Presidents on Mount Rushmore

Test Fifteen Answer 39
Budapest

Test Fifteen Answer 40
Over and out

Test Fifteen Answer 41
turn / tern

Test Fifteen Answer 42
driver, wheels

Test Fifteen Answer 43
kingfisher, canary, robin

Test Fifteen Answer 44
DILLTU + EFGH = delightful

Test Fifteen Answer 45
bobcat

Test Fifteen Answer 46
none the wiser

Test Fifteen Answer 47
orange

Test Fifteen Answer 48
6 pockets on a pool table

Test Fifteen Answer 49
idea - perception

Test Fifteen Answer 50
rise and shine

Test Sixteen Answer 1
sent, scent

Test Sixteen Answer 2
MARSUPIAL - primulas
NOVELTIES - novelist

Test Sixteen Answer 3
serene

Test Sixteen Answer 4
rapscallion - rascal
recline - lie
regulates - rules

Test Sixteen Answer 5
stash cash

Test Sixteen Answer 6
beach / beech

Test Sixteen Answer 7
thin on top
come to a head

Test Sixteen Answer 8
almost

Test Sixteen Answer 9
7 Brides for Seven Brothers

Test Sixteen Answer 10
methodical, disorderly

Test Sixteen Answer 11
inc(andes)cense

Test Sixteen Answer 12
revolution – revolt, rotund - round
salvage - save

Test Sixteen Answer 13
senile felines

Test Sixteen Answer 14
pull a fast one

Test Sixteen Answer 15
state - federation

Test Sixteen Answer 16
SOCCER

Test Sixteen Answer 17
slip of the pen

Test Sixteen Answer 18
mauve

Test Sixteen Answer 19
far and wide
ever and anon

Test Sixteen Answer 20
hooked, aquiline

Test Sixteen Answer 21
EIOPPR + STUV = supportive

Test Sixteen Answer 22
14 lines in a sonnet

Test Sixteen Answer 23
creek / creak

Test Sixteen Answer 24
undo - disentangle

Test Sixteen Answer 25
All in all

Test Sixteen Answer 26
tarpon

Test Sixteen Answer 27
root

Test Sixteen Answer 28
Liken – compare

Test Sixteen Answer 29
(c)   Medicine

Test Sixteen Answer 30
Stone: all words can be prefixed with fruits
i.e. applecart, banana split, dateline, plumage,
limestone

Test Sixteen Answer 31
OMBUDSMAN - summoned
PIROUETTE - treetop

Test Sixteen Answer 32
OUT

Test Sixteen Answer 33
ma(gnat)e

Test Sixteen Answer 34
verve - enthusiasm

Test Sixteen Answer 35
fawn / faun

Test Sixteen Answer 36
define

Test Sixteen Answer 37
roomy moor

Test Sixteen Answer 38
Ascension

Test Sixteen Answer 39
never say die
wine and dine

Test Sixteen Answer 40
19 to the dozen

Test Sixteen Answer 41
river bank, water

Test Sixteen Answer 42
as large as life

Test Sixteen Answer 43
Afghan

Test Sixteen Answer 44
here and now, home and dry

Test Sixteen Answer 45
Portrait

Test Sixteen Answer 46
oval - elliptical

Test Sixteen Answer 47
Ant: to produce: pageant, anthem, hemline, lineage

Test Sixteen Answer 48
8 kings of England called Henry

Test Sixteen Answer 49
A thing of beauty is a joy for ever.

Test Sixteen Answer 50
Plan today (or plot today)

Test Seventeen Answer 1
Manitoba

Test Seventeen Answer 2
AAEIOPT + KLMN = kleptomania

Test Seventeen Answer 3
instance / instants

Test Seventeen Answer 4
Purify, befoul

Test Seventeen Answer 5
QUALIFIED - quailed
REPREHEND - preened

Test Seventeen Answer 6
sighing

Test Seventeen Answer 7
NNNN + ACEEMOTU = announcement

Test Seventeen Answer 8
preface, appendix

Test Seventeen Answer 9
heads will roll

Test Seventeen Answer 10
seer - soothsayer

Test Seventeen Answer 11
kith and kin
nip and tuck

Test Seventeen Answer 12
hijack

Test Seventeen Answer 13
coyote, baboon, impala

Test Seventeen Answer 14
erupt pure

Test Seventeen Answer 15
Primrose

Test Seventeen Answer 16
JOCKEY

Test Seventeen Answer 17
Synonyms: irrational, unsound
Antonym: judicious

Test Seventeen Answer 18
gratuity, endowment

Test Seventeen Answer 19
15 minutes of fame per person

Test Seventeen Answer 20
Estonia and England

Test Seventeen Answer 21
not on your life

Test Seventeen Answer 22
calmness

Test Seventeen Answer 23
step / steppe

Test Seventeen Answer 24
arm in arm
cut it out

Test Seventeen Answer 25
IN

Test Seventeen Answer 26
somnolent

Test Seventeen Answer 27
SIGNIFIED - dignifies; TURBULENT - blunter

Test Seventeen Answer 28
Trimester

Test Seventeen Answer 29
satisfied – sated, separate – part, splotches - spots
supervisor - superior

Test Seventeen Answer 30
(c)   Haddock

Test Seventeen Answer 31
short shrift   -   shrift = confession
rank and file   -   rank = row
out of kilter   -   kilter = order

Test Seventeen Answer 32
sodium chlorate - none of the others repeats a letter.

Test Seventeen Answer 33
scales

Test Seventeen Answer 34
the middle of nowhere. Each one describes successive letters of the alphabet:

first of **a**ll
starting **b**lock
a fifth of s**c**otch
the end of the worl**d**
the beginning of the **e**nd
starting **f**riction
the middle of the ni**g**ht
the middle of now**h**ere

Test Seventeen Answer 35
Helicopter

Test Seventeen Answer 36
ZZZZ + AIP = pizzazz

Test Seventeen Answer 37
sooth

Test Seventeen Answer 38
abbess, access

Test Seventeen Answer 39
fast

Test Seventeen Answer 40
Being wise after the event

Test Seventeen Answer 41
Truce: each word begins with the second and fifth letters of the previous word.

Test Seventeen Answer 42
10 frames in ten pin bowling

Test Seventeen Answer 43
eyes, legs

Test Seventeen Answer 44
Tree and black. The words in the first column can all be suffixed with top and the words in the second column can be suffixed with bottom.

Test Seventeen Answer 45
See eye to eye

Test Seventeen Answer 46
Propriety, decorum

Test Seventeen Answer 47
FILL WIDE = wildlife

The types of deer are antelope (one leapt), brocket (trek cob) and reindeer (dire erne)

Test Seventeen Answer 48
Side-effect

Test Seventeen Answer 49
They contain four letters that appear side by side in order (backwards or forwards) on a standard QWERTY keyboard i.e. S(TREW)N, PROP(ERTY)

Test Seventeen Answer 50
poor droop

Test Eighteen Answer 1
rite / right

Test Eighteen Answer 2
canopy

Test Eighteen Answer 3
Eclipse and marmalade
All words contain body parts which are in order from top to bottom of the body, apart from marmalade and eclipse: Conv(eye)r, m(arm)alade, ec(lip)se, te(leg)ram, pho(toe)lectric

Test Eighteen Answer 4
Br(east)bone

Test Eighteen Answer 5
RAM. So that read backwards *Mary had a little lamb* appears

Test Eighteen Answer 6
retract pact

Test Eighteen Answer 7
ravenous, satisfied

Test Eighteen Answer 8
jig - prance

Test Eighteen Answer 9
thirsty

Test Eighteen Answer 10
play hard to get

Test Eighteen Answer 11
party trap

Test Eighteen Answer 12
school

Test Eighteen Answer 13
come and get it
far and wide

Test Eighteen Answer 14
step out of line

Test Eighteen Answer 15
BATTLE

Test Eighteen Answer 16
Lay down the law

Test Eighteen Answer 17
Ewe, you

Test Eighteen Answer 18
UNIVERSAL - unravels
VENTILATE - levitate

Test Eighteen Answer 19
Peace, truce

Test Eighteen Answer 20
astute

Test Eighteen Answer 21
obviate, avert

Test Eighteen Answer 22
16 pawns on a chess board

Test Eighteen Answer 23
Fine

Test Eighteen Answer 24
2 minims in a whole note

Test Eighteen Answer 25
Happy

Test Eighteen Answer 26
seven eves

Test Eighteen Answer 27
(d)   Water-fly

Test Eighteen Answer 28
SEA

Test Eighteen Answer 29
ABRIN = brain

Test Eighteen Answer 30
Photo-opportunity

Test Eighteen Answer 31
XYZ = rip: ripple, tripod, script, regrip

Test Eighteen Answer 32
Centre of attraction

Test Eighteen Answer 33
Son

Test Eighteen Answer 34
WINDSWEPT – stipend; XYLORIMBA - mailbox

Test Eighteen Answer 35
understudy

Test Eighteen Answer 36
drawn onward

Test Eighteen Answer 37
bearing / baring

Test Eighteen Answer 38
messenger

Test Eighteen Answer 39
alter/alert/later

Test Eighteen Answer 40
to be or not to be

Test Eighteen Answer 41
water, land

Test Eighteen Answer 42
kit and kaboodle-   kaboodle = collection
footpad   -   pad = highwayman
raring to go   -   raring = enthusiastic

Test Eighteen Answer 43
Taken a second bite of the cherry.

Test Eighteen Answer 44
K(EROS)ENE

Test Eighteen Answer 45
walls have ears

Test Eighteen Answer 46
Can

Test Eighteen Answer 47
Cultivated, suave, sophisticated, urbane, refined

Test Eighteen Answer 48
PUT to produce deputy, repute, compute, reputed

Test Eighteen Answer 49
serve/sever/veers

Test Eighteen Answer 50
feign / fain

Test Nineteen Answer 1
Set up shop

Test Nineteen Answer 2
RSTU: prosecute

Test Nineteen Answer 3
Ermine

Test Nineteen Answer 4
lay

Test Nineteen Answer 5
Mint, basil, sage

Test Nineteen Answer 6
DOC: they are the first two and last letters of each of the seven dwarfs; Dopey, Bashful, Sneezy, Sleepy, Happy, Grumpy, Doc

Test Nineteen Answer 7
Add AEIOU to produce: paramount, forehead, manifold, cormorant, permutable.

Test Nineteen Answer 8
Feudal: the words begin with the first two letters of October, November, December, January, February.

Test Nineteen Answer 9
B(ROAD)CAST

Test Nineteen Answer 10
patient

Test Nineteen Answer 11
300 for a perfect score in ten-pin bowling

Test Nineteen Answer 12
sever, join

Test Nineteen Answer 13
Prototype

Test Nineteen Answer 14
AIRBUS

Test Nineteen Answer 15
Cog –ratchet

Test Nineteen Answer 16
AILM + RSTU = altruism

Test Nineteen Answer 17
future, former

Test Nineteen Answer 18
Whistling while I work

Test Nineteen Answer 19
Just

Test Nineteen Answer 20
saunter, ramble

Test Nineteen Answer 21
AT

Test Nineteen Answer 22
IIIII + BLNSTVY = invisibility

Test Nineteen Answer 23
Roundelay

Test Nineteen Answer 24
Add TIT FOR TAT to produce stitch, before, static

Test Nineteen Answer 25
battler, babbler

Test Nineteen Answer 26
Founder

Test Nineteen Answer 27
Ascribe, coaster, ecstasy, special

Test Nineteen Answer 28
Global, international, universal, worldwide

Test Nineteen Answer 29
(b)   Of the gums

Test Nineteen Answer 30
Win (no-win, winnow)

Test Nineteen Answer 31
MNOP: champion

Test Nineteen Answer 32
EGHOORR + TUVW = overwrought

Test Nineteen Answer 33
Phobia, liking

Test Nineteen Answer 34
TTTT + AEESU = statuette

Test Nineteen Answer 35
crook, creek

Test Nineteen Answer 36
AALN + BCDE = balanced

Test Nineteen Answer 37
CDEF: edifice

Test Nineteen Answer 38
perseverence

Test Nineteen Answer 39
Chaste, chased

Test Nineteen Answer 40
KOPR + ABCD = backdrop

Test Nineteen Answer 41
gold

Test Nineteen Answer 42
pages, letters

Test Nineteen Answer 43
Room: all words can be prefixed with ball

Test Nineteen Answer 44
PQRS: perquisite

Test Nineteen Answer 45
Damage, repair

Test Nineteen Answer 46
LLLL + AEGIY = illegally

Test Nineteen Answer 47
Alfresco, amnesiac, escalate, semantic

Test Nineteen Answer 48
Lace – places

Test Nineteen Answer 49
teach speech

Test Nineteen Answer 50
Mutual Admiration Society

Test Twenty Answer 1
edge - boundary

Test Twenty Answer 2
7 players in a water polo team

Test Twenty Answer 3
Part: partridge, partner, parties

Test Twenty Answer 4
Cart

Test Twenty Answer 5
YODELLING - yelling
ZOOLOGIST - igloos

Test Twenty Answer 6
Tough –ought

Test Twenty Answer 7
Redolent, aromatic

Test Twenty Answer 8
Heaven: the words proceed first aid, second wind, third world, fourth estate, fifth column, sixth sense, seventh heaven.

Test Twenty Answer 9
slime/smile/miles

Test Twenty Answer 10
solemnise, profane

Test Twenty Answer 11
Fit – capable

Test Twenty Answer 12
usual - customary

Test Twenty Answer 13
hall / haul

Test Twenty Answer 14
year in year out

Test Twenty Answer 15
PETULA

Test Twenty Answer 16
series - progression

Test Twenty Answer 17
now and then, over and out

Test Twenty Answer 18
wax - increase

Test Twenty Answer 19
kilns/slink/links

Test Twenty Answer 20
touch and go, wait and see

Test Twenty Answer 21
midsummer madness

Test Twenty Answer 22
invade / inveighed

Test Twenty Answer 23
lampoon, satirise

Test Twenty Answer 24
The Russian Revolution

Test Twenty Answer 25
air - atmosphere

Test Twenty Answer 26
fir

Test Twenty Answer 27
PLAY

Test Twenty Answer 28
reset/steer/trees

Test Twenty Answer 29
Light – flighty

Test Twenty Answer 30
(a)   Fish

Test Twenty Answer 31
citadel and dialect

Test Twenty Answer 32
Al**lege**, ve**toe**s, d**rib**ble, s**ear**ch, w**arm**ly, cal**lip**er, ob**eye**d, ar**gum**ent, w**hip**ped

Test Twenty Answer 33
change of heart
forget me not
hall of mirrors

Test Twenty Answer 34
woe - heartache

Test Twenty Answer 35
raise / rays

Test Twenty Answer 36
absent without leave
all in all
three day event

Test Twenty Answer 37
train
mail **train**
s**train**ing
train bearer
res**train**t

Test Twenty Answer 38
random access, Indian summer, armour plated,
spinal column, tunnel vision

Test Twenty Answer 39
walls have ears
turn the tables
time after time

Test Twenty Answer 40
numbers, works

Test Twenty Answer 41
petal/plate/leapt

Test Twenty Answer 42
land

Test Twenty Answer 43
surge / serge

Test Twenty Answer 44
subcontinental

Test Twenty Answer 45
All form another word when beheaded:
c/hastening, v/indication, r/evolution,
e/motionless, p/raise, b/rain

Test Twenty Answer 46
The meaning of the last word in the abbreviation
is repeated each time, for example DC current =
direct current current
LCD display = liquid crystal display display

Test Twenty Answer 47
sound = soundless, soundness
base = baseless, baseness
wit = witless, witness

Test Twenty Answer 48
bank teller — tell = to count
swashbuckler — swash = bluster or stagger,
— buckler = small shield
to and fro — fro = from

Test Twenty Answer 49
intact

Test Twenty Answer 50
1000 word puzzles in this book